FEELS
LIKE
HOME

FEELS LIKE HOME

A SONG FOR THE SONORAN BORDERLANDS

LINDA RONSTADT AND LAWRENCE DOWNES

PHOTOGRAPHS BY BILL STEEN

HEYDAY
BERKELEY, CALIFORNIA

Front endsheet: View of the Río Sonora Valley from above the town of Baviácora, Sonora.

Back endsheet: Besides Criollo cattle, 47 Ranch also raises sheep for wool.

Library of Congress Cataloging-in-Publication Data

Names: Ronstadt, Linda, author. | Downes, Lawrence, author. | Steen, Bill, photographer.
Title: Feels like home : a song for the Sonoran borderlands / by Linda Ronstadt and Lawrence Downes, photographs by Bill Steen.
Description: Berkeley, California : Heyday, [2022] | Where the water turns -- Desert people -- Margarita's letters -- Mi pueblo -- A love story -- La frontera -- The mission garden -- Canelo diary -- Desert cattle -- El futuro -- Coda: my dream
Identifiers: LCCN 2021060716 (print) | LCCN 2021060717 (ebook) | ISBN 9781597145794 (hardcover) | ISBN 1597145793 (hardcover) | ISBN 9781597145800 (epub)
Subjects: LCSH: Ronstadt, Linda. | Singers--United States--Biography. | Mexican-American Border Region--Civilization. | Mexican American cooking. | LCGFT: Autobiographies.
Classification: LCC ML420.R8753 A3 2022 (print) | LCC ML420.R8753 (ebook) | DDC 782.42164092 [B]--dc23
LC record available at https://lccn.loc.gov/2021060716
LC ebook record available at https://lccn.loc.gov/2021060717

Front cover design: Amy Dakos/Kosh Design Studios
Front cover typography and interior design/typesetting: Ashley Ingram
Design coordinator and photo archivist: Genny Schorr
Cover photography: Gilbert Ronstadt

Published by Heyday
P.O. Box 9145, Berkeley, California 94709
(510) 549-3564
heydaybooks.com

Printed in China by Imago

10 9 8 7 6 5 4 3 2

For Annabelle

The Ronstadt family at home in Tucson about 1953: Ruth Mary lounging at left, Gilbert holding baby Mike, Suzy holding a kitten, and Peter yelling at Linda.

Feels like home to me.
Feels like I'm all the way back
Where I come from.
Feels like I'm all the way back
Where I belong.

—RANDY NEWMAN, "Feels Like Home"

Vámonos muriendo juntos.
Que me entierren en tu suelo.
Y seremos dos difuntos,
Rodeados de mil recuerdos.

—LALO GUERRERO, "Barrio Viejo"

A Ronstadt and Dalton family picnic in the fall of 1903. Linda's grandfather Fred, holding guitar at right, only has eyes for Lupe Dalton, who's lounging and smiling. (They married a few months later.) Also, from left: Hortense Ronstadt with baby Marguerite, Henry Dalton, Matilde Ronstadt holding baby Helen, Armand Ronstadt, Dick Ronstadt (holding rifle), Maria Jesus Dalton, and Louise Dalton. José María Ronstadt took the photo.

CONTENTS

July's fierce monsoon rains cast rainbows over the mountains near Bacoachi and paint the Sonoran Desert green.

INTRODUCTION
Lawrence Downes

THIS BOOK MEANDERED INTO EXISTENCE, taking shape from several long conversations I had with Linda Ronstadt, starting in 2009, first by phone and then in a succession of vehicles, each one, oddly, larger than the last. First a car and then a minivan and finally a bus, a full-sized motorcoach sailing down an Arizona highway, the Sonoran Desert rolling by. We also spoke while stationary: on a park bench in Mexico and a few times at Linda's home in San Francisco, me with my recorder on a sofa and she holding forth from an adjacent chaise. But mostly these were rambling interviews; they were done while rambling.

We talked about Linda's family: her mom and dad and grandparents, her sister and two brothers, her two kids and many cousins. We talked about horses and other childhood pets, her family's hardware store, old boyfriends, Catholic school. We talked about comforting things, like bread-baking, tamale-making, and burrito-folding, and frightening ones, like the wild desert after dark and the way cottonwood trees can murderously drop their limbs and crush things without warning, like the one that flattened Linda's bedroom when she was a girl. (Luckily, she was elsewhere.)

Once we were riding on a dark desert highway in northern Mexico. We were listening to Linda's albums, a request from me that she had at first declined, then hesitantly granted, then seemed to enjoy, providing live commentary for each track. "This song's a bitch to sing," she said at one point. "It makes me tired just thinking about it." When we got to her version of "Carmelita," Warren Zevon's desolate song about being strung out and suicidal on the outskirts of town, she started laughing. "Am I pretty convincing as a gun-toting heroin addict? Are you buying that?" That trip, in 2013, became an article in the *New York Times*, "Linda Ronstadt's Borderland," which reads now as a dry run for this book.

Those travels flipped my understanding of Linda inside out. It can be surprising to think how much of her work is waterborne, even nautical, summoning ships, swamps, and sea foam. A blue bayou, with those fishing boats with their sails afloat. A shattered heart on a sinking ship out in mid-ocean. Her wary sideways glance toward a shadowy horse hastening down the beach in Malibu. I'd even add pirates, climbing the rigging out in Penzance.

But now I also think of a little girl growing up where the ground got too hot to walk on. Her solution: dipping her bare soles over and over in water and dust until they were caked in clay. In her mud huaraches, she could go anywhere. This was Tucson, which Linda left as a teenager, though she was always able to go home, and home again, because that place and her people gave her a rock-solid identity she never lost.

This is the Linda who in the 1980s made a record of old Mexican songs that became the best-selling non-English-language album ever. The Linda who, in 2010, marched through the streets of Phoenix with her old friend Dolores Huerta and ten thousand immigrant laborers to deplore a sheriff who brutalized Mexicans and other brown people in Arizona. And the Linda who, in 2019, told the United States secretary of state—to his face at a celebratory dinner at the State Department—to stop enabling an immigrant-hating president.

This book aims to show another Linda, to give you another portrait to place on your mental mantle beside the ones of her singing at the Troubadour or hanging with the Eagles or Dolly or Emmylou or Jerry Brown or Kermit. This is Linda before L.A., before stadium rock, before any Grammys, and with real ponies, not Stone ones. This is little Linda, Mexican Linda, cowgirl Linda, desert Linda.

Also sibling Linda. Older brother Peter is in this book, with stories to tell. So are Linda's late sister and brother, Suzy and Mike. I was lucky to have met Suzy in 2013 at the house Linda still had then in Tucson. Suzy had dropped by to take some garden thing of Linda's away in her pickup truck. She had long silver hair and a warm laugh. "I miss my sister," she said to me, speaking in the direction of Linda. Suzy died in 2015. I never met Mike, the youngest sibling, who died in 2016 and was by everyone's account an all-around lovely guy. He stayed in Tucson, leading a band and raising musical sons and making a ton of good homegrown music.

Talk about rambling: This historical-musical-edible memoir started out as a cookbook, Arizona-themed, that was somehow going to include Sandra Day O'Connor, Barry Goldwater, and Muhammad Ali, whose name is on a Parkinson's disease research center in Phoenix. Linda's friend CC Goldwater, Barry's granddaughter, had the idea. Linda emailed me to ask for help in writing it, since her condition—she has progressive supranuclear palsy, whose symptoms are similar to Parkinson's—made it hard to type, much less do all the heavy lifting a book requires.

My first answer was, "Yes of course," and my second was, *Say what now?* "It could possibly turn into great fun," Linda wrote. She was right about the fun, though the cookbook idea didn't gel. Still, the road trips kept happening, because we knew we had something too good not to share. Between all the Linda memories to tell, Ronstadts to meet, songs to hear, places to discover, and things to eat, out there between Tucson and Sonora, there was a book to make.

We are both grateful to Heyday, and to Steve Wasserman, its publisher, who was Linda's agent for her 2013 memoir, *Simple Dreams*, and who understood what this book could be. He stuck with us and we worked it out and here we are.

There's a lot in these pages about how a singer is both born and made, learning by singing and being sung to. Linda's grandfather Fred was a bandleader, and her dad, Gilbert, also had the Ronstadt gift—he could have sung professionally, like his friend Lalo Guerrero, the Chicano music legend and old Tucsonan. Linda remembers Lalo and her dad serenading her on her birthday, when she was three. She remembers her dad's singing voice wowing everyone who heard it, even the tableside mariachis in Mexican restaurants.

And speaking of restaurants, Linda also remembers a lot about growing up with beans, tamales, chiles, and melted cheese. Her food memories are exquisite, even carnal, and though she mainly goes for healthful fish and fruits and vegetables these days, when she tells you about butter from a hot Tucson cheese crisp dripping down her chin, or the silken chew of a tortilla made with lard, you will be delighted to meet *that* Linda, too. Linda is not known for her kitchen work; the most complicated thing she cooks for herself these days is toast, although she used to bake whole-wheat bread in her hippie days, using a recipe she adapted from the *Fannie Farmer Cookbook*, with wheat gluten and honey and molasses. She made it often enough to know it by heart. She put a photo of a loaf she made on the back cover of her 1995 album, *Feels Like Home*.

When Linda and I tried to replicate it, we came up with some decent loaves, though they weren't precisely what she remembered, so she decided not to include the recipe here. What we did re-create here is a Ronstadt road trip, the real deal, led by herself and joined by her family members and dear friends from back in the day. She's gotten the band together and gone back on the road—without the sex and drugs (sorry) and with corridos, rancheras, and huapangos instead of rock-and-roll. The guest musicians this time include Mockingbirds, not Eagles, and a lot of Ronstadts. And while I wish there were a way to include a lot more of Ry Cooder and Randy Newman in this story, there isn't; their place in Linda's life lies a little outside the Tucson-Sonora penumbra.

Besides Linda's family, there are her childhood friends like Katya Peterson, who is doing her best to keep Tucson a spirited, welcoming, and decent place. Katya's late mother, Cele, a fashion designer and entrepreneur who made the most of an incredible century of living, is in this book, too. So is Bob Vint, an architect who is guiding the renovation of the San Xavier del Bac mission outside Tucson, an exquisite living link to the region's deep history. And the ranchers Deb and Dennis Moroney, who are doing their own kind of historical revitalization, raising vintage Criollo cattle in McNeal.

The people in this book have been in Linda's life a long time. They are both close to her heart and close to home. If you want to know who Linda is and how she got that way, these are the folks who can tell you, and they are excellent company for the journey ahead. Now let's talk about where we're going.

This book is about a place, a particular stretch of southern Arizona and northern Mexico, the people and things within it, how it has changed over time, and—maybe more important—how it has stayed the same. If you put a pencil on a map near Tucson, Arizona, and drew a line curving down into Mexico and around the meandering length of the Sonora River, the Río Sonora, and back up to where you started, you will make an oval that contains almost everything that happens in this book.

There is no official name for the land within this line, no boundary markers, no fixed coordinates to establish this area—about 250 miles from top to bottom, and 150 side to side—as a geographical or political artifact. It straddles two countries, after all. But it is nonetheless its own coherent and congruous region, with a distinctive history and prehistory, its own cast of historical figures and peoples, and with many things that live and grow and are seen and made and eaten here and no place else. The singularity of this territory—call it the Sonoran borderlands—fits nicely with the purposes of this book, which aims to introduce you to the part of the world that, more than any other in Linda Ronstadt's life, feels to her like home.

This is it: the oval you just drew.

It's mostly desert, hot and dry most of the year, but it also includes mountain ranges and forests, valleys and mesas, rivers and streams—or at least the channels and troughs where water used to go. Many waterways here, like the Santa Cruz River through Tucson, are intermittently or permanently dry. Many other lines crisscross this territory—roads and train tracks and highways, Interstates 19 and 10, plus other, older pathways that were made and followed by humans for centuries or millennia but long ago were buried under blacktop.

Humans have lived continuously in this area for thousands of years, despite its harshness and heat, and their routes across it tend to be laid on top of one another. The ways people choose to get across this land of thorn and stone tend to be the most direct and efficient ones, such as where a pass cuts through an otherwise implacable wall of mountains, or where water is relatively close, or where the terrain is reasonably flat and clear. This applies whether you are an Indigenous Sonoran following a

LEFT: Sonora is a paradox: a fertile desert, both dry and green. **RIGHT:** In slanting sunlight, the thorny landscape glows.

footpath a thousand years ago, a sixteenth-century Spaniard on horseback, or a guy driving a semitrailer of tomatoes up through Nogales.

The region includes living things, too, dizzying in their diversity. Gnarly and scaly desert creatures that keep a low profile in burrows and under rocks, and surreal flashy ones that get in your face, like the palo verde trees, whose trunks are bright green and whose yellow blossoms explode across the desert in spring, and the cactuses shaped like barrels, broomsticks, organ pipes, ping-pong paddles, and tall skinny people, lifting their hallelujah arms to the heavens. Living beside these and among all the mesquite trees are the docile livestock—cattle and horses and goats—and the friendly, non-prickly crops that live only to serve, like alfalfa, favas, garlic, wheat, squash, beans, agave, and chiles.

And finally, your oval encloses a large number of the most important people in Linda's life, living and dead, people whose family ties to this region are old and deep. The region abounds in humans who are as firmly rooted as desert plants. They include the Indigenous peoples of various tribes and bands, whose stories are older than written history; Mexicans, descended from Indigenous peoples and from Spaniards, many of whom in Sonora trace their ancestry to the Basque lands of northern Spain; the descendants of Chinese immigrants from the nineteenth century; and Americans of mixed Mexican and European ancestry, like the Ronstadts.

The border is the line that runs right through the heart of this book, slicing Arizona and Mexico apart. It is an unavoidable part of the landscape, though there is nothing human or organic about it. It climbs and perches absurdly on rocky hilltops and slashes through remote and ecologically pristine desert. Where it meets highways and passes through towns like Nogales and Naco, the line declares itself with rusted steel columns, concrete embankments, floodlights, and concertina wire. The barrier is meant to crush any hope of crossing, and the rows of razor coils make it lethal to try.

This book is about crossing that line, and recrossing and crisscrossing it until it fades to insignificance, like a rubbed-out pencil mark. If not for that jagged scar, this would be a book without borders. It inhabits both sides of the line, containing about equal parts Arizona and Mexico. Its edges are fluid, natural, often invisible, drawn partly in earth and desert sky and partly in memory.

If this book were a radio signal, you might first pick it up on an Arizona highway, well south of Phoenix, coming into the glow of Linda's hometown. It would be playing something old and Mexican, from a time when the border was a more agreeable place. It might be the ranchera idol Lola Beltrán, or maybe Trío Calaveras, the huapango kings, or Trío Tariácuri, courting, swooning, and sweetly grieving, with songs like "El Sueño," The Dream.

Ya me cansé de soñar.	*I'm tired of dreaming.*
El sueño me hace sufrir.	*The dream makes me suffer.*
Quisiera que al despertar,	*I wish that when I woke up,*
Mi sueño fuera verdad	*My dream was true*
Para dejar de sufrir.	*To stop suffering.*

Me acuesto pensando en ti,	*I go to bed thinking of you,*
Y en mi sueño estás conmigo.	*And in my dream you are with me.*
Y me siento tan feliz,	*And I feel so happy,*
Al soñar que estoy contigo.	*Dreaming that I am with you.*

Linda and her brothers, Peter and Mike, sang "El Sueño" on a record in 1991, using the same harmonies they had worked out as kids in Tucson in the 1950s and '60s. Growing up in that place and time, the Ronstadt siblings—those three plus Suzy—were as likely to absorb Mexican folk tunes into their bodies as Mexican frijoles, barbacoa, and chilaquiles. Huapangos were as familiar to them as Hank Williams and operetta and rock-and-roll.

Tucson is the part of Arizona where the general orientation of life, in its flavor and spirit, turns southward, toward Mexico, toward something older, slower, more earthen, less determined to vanquish the desert than to live decently within it. If Phoenix, the capital, is a moon crater with golf, Tucson is a canyon full of cottonwoods, with some Ronstadts singing "El Sueño" in the dappled shade.

The public first knew Linda as a dark-eyed singer with a German last name who sang folk rock out of California. Many learned of her Mexican roots only later, in 1987, when she released *Canciones de Mi Padre*, an album of huapangos, corridos, rancheras, and other old-style music she had grown up with. She had illustrious mariachis accompanying her and an ability to sing in Spanish that could have fooled you into thinking she was somebody's cousin from Hermosillo.

Ronstadt's Mexican record was dismissed and patronized by some critics who didn't get it. ("A fascinating bit of eccentricity from a most unlikely source," said *Rolling Stone*.) But a generation of Mexican Americans bought the record and its 1991 successor, *Mas Canciones*, by the millions, and in the listening and re-listening and savoring and sharing, something changed—in the broader culture and in themselves.

"Our generation would become the first group of Mexican Americans to grow up comfortable with both sides of that term," wrote the journalist Gustavo Arellano in the *Los Angeles Times* in 2017. His article was headlined "Linda Ronstadt's 'Canciones de Mi Padre' changed my life, and my culture."

"Seeing Ronstadt sing in Spanish on national television, her album cover published in newspapers, taught us that it was OK to be unapologetically Mexican, no matter how assimilated we may be," Arellano wrote. Referring to the Mexicanized nickname for L.A.'s baseball team, he added: "Any time you hear one of us say 'Doyers,' or wear a splendid guayabera, it's because of her."

Linda's Mexican records helped a generation find and embrace its mexicanidad. But where did Linda find hers? That is what we are here to explore. Up and down and there and back, never mind the border.

Linda left Tucson at eighteen, but it never left her.

Find that radio frequency again and turn it up. You'll hear it bell-clear as you drive all over Tucson and as you keep driving south. Let the Trío Tariácuri sing you past the city limits and onto the Tohono O'odham reservation, past the San Xavier del Bac mission and the Desert Diamond casino, past the highway-side suburbs and scrub and the tented Border Patrol checkpoint, and on into Nogales, Arizona. On the far edge of town: the border wall. It juts into the desert in both directions from the north-south highway like the long arms of a crucifix.

Beyond the wall is Mexican Sonora, buzzing with as many Ronstadt family lives and histories as on this side. The breach in the land does not breach the continuity of this story. It's the same territory, the same sunlight and heat and monsoon rains, just with a longer horizon across space and time.

This book overlaps with much of the Sonoran Desert, but not all of it. It matches up well with the habitat of the saguaro cactus, which, like Linda, is particular about where it likes to live and how much cold it tolerates. But it also extends to places

Saguaros live in the Sonoran Desert and nowhere else. Deep-rooted and slow to grow, they can survive for centuries.

Even in a place so parched and hot, life is defiant. Cactuses climb bare, rocky slopes where they have no business being.

where the land rises higher than the saguaros' range—to the archipelagoes of "sky islands," cooler, wetter mountaintops whose plants and animals live isolated from the hot, dry ocean of lower desert.

The fixed terrain of this book is social, too, peopled with characters with distinct ways of viewing the world. Sonoran life, south and north of the border, in a land of heat and little rain, survives and thrives through cooperation and interdependence. Cowboying is hard. Ranching can be perilous. Beauty and comfort often must be conjured from unlikely, unforgiving places.

As Linda's grandfather Federico José María Ronstadt, who was born in 1868 and went by Fred, demonstrates in his austere memoir, *Borderman*, published posthumously in 1993, surviving in Sonora meant you made what you used and fixed what you broke and grew what you ate. In Sonora, agave and mesquite and emory oak cover the land and don't resemble food as many of us recognize it. But what they

When this map, showing the new international border, was published in 1858, my great-grandfather was a reserve army officer in Sonora, and my great-grandmother was a girl of nine, living in Altar.

yield is exquisite: the local mescal called bacanora, and edible bean pods and acorns, the latter also called bellotas.

The people in this book know horses and dress like cowboys. They chew mesquite beans and barbecue over mesquite fires and turn mesquite posts and wire into low, indestructible fencing. They melt cheese into their frijoles and they air-dry beef in papery sheets and stone-pound it into fluffy machaca, preservable until it can be reborn with oil and onions and tomatoes and eggs and fiery flakes of dried chiltepín chiles.

They sound like inhabitants of the nineteenth century, but these ways live on in the twenty-first century, too. Bring all the dead ones back and invite them to a pachanga, a Sonoran ranchers' picnic. Everybody would have a lot to talk about: the weather, the horses, the cooking, the music. They would love the same food and know the same songs. Maybe somebody would play some tunes on the Martin guitar that has been in Linda's family since 1898. Linda's grandfather bought it new and played it his whole life. Linda got it from her dad when she left home to be a singer, and many years later she entrusted it to her nephew Petie.

Here's what these ancient borderlands have in common, from Tucson to Nogales to the southern stretches of Sonora, about a day's drive south of the border, and from the flanks of the Sierra Madre Occidental mountain range in the east to the sunset-pink waters of the Sea of Cortés in the west: To Linda, they feel like home.

These are the natural boundaries that define the range of this otherwise borderless book.

But where, you ask, is the center, the source, the wellspring? Where is the radio signal coming from?

From Banámichi, on the Río Sonora.

A NOTE FROM LINDA ON THE FOOD

Most of the recipes in this book are native to Sonora and southern Arizona. Some are ancient and obscure, like tepary beans; others are up-to-date and highly localized, like Sonoran hot dogs and Tucson cheese crisps. Many of the traditional dishes come from the kitchens of excellent home cooks who live along the Río Sonora, including Armida Contreras of the village of La Estancia and Lupita Madero of Bacoachi.

For a few fundamental recipes, we've gratefully adapted methods and tips from authors who are deeply respected for translating Mexican home cooking for American kitchens: Diana Kennedy, Rick Bayless (Frijoles de la Olla, Frijoles Refritos), and Pati Jinich (Carne Asada). For our discussion of untamed crops like wild greens and agave, we bow to the expertise of the ethnobotanist and writer Gary Paul Nabhan, our friend in Patagonia, whose study of native foods and Indigenous cultures won him the MacArthur "genius" grant in 1990. He understands desert nutrition and deliciousness better than anybody.

As for the Ronstadt recipes, these are the real ones that I grew up with and that have reappeared at holidays and other family gatherings for generations. Who knows when and where we first got them, but they have been faithfully protected and passed on by the cooks in our family, especially my lovely sister-in-law Jackie. To her, and my grandma and grandpa, and my mom and dad, and whoever showed young Fred Ronstadt more than a century ago how to bake a sweet calabaza in a homemade adobe oven—gracias.

Many of the ingredients can be hard or impossible to find in stores or markets outside Sonora and Arizona, but you can find them online. One good place to buy chiltepín chiles, tepary beans, and other elements of a well-stocked Sonoran pantry is nativeseeds.org, the website of Native Seeds/SEARCH, a Tucson nonprofit dedicated to finding and saving the seeds and crops of the Southwest.

Now to define some terms. "Lard" in these recipes means pork lard, an essential ingredient if you want beans and flour tortillas to taste right. Diana Kennedy, in *The Art of Mexican Cooking*, says it's okay—even preferable—to use vegetable shortening when making large Sonoran-style flour tortillas. I'm not here to argue, but I still believe in lard.

Kennedy and I do agree on this: We both disdain kosher salt and consider it an enemy of flavor. "Salt" here means sea salt.

Spring onions are scallions with bigger bulbs. They have a lovely, strong oniony flavor and are easy to find in Latino groceries, as is Mexican oregano, which is better for these recipes than the Mediterranean kind. Mexican crema is a staple condiment, tangier and a little thinner than sour cream, and it is a wonderful finishing touch on beans, tacos, and especially Sonoran hot dogs. Queso fresco, "fresh cheese," is white, mild, and easily crumbled. It won't melt away to goo in your Sonoran cheese soup. That soup is best made with Sonora's local cheese—queso regional de Sonora—but queso fresco will do. Anaheim chiles are a great border-crossing chile, popular across the Southwest and northern Mexico. They are about six inches long and not terribly hot, but deliciously essential, whether fresh and green or dried and red. Anaheim chiles, California chiles, New Mexico chiles, or Hatch chiles (for the famous chile-growing town in New Mexico)—these are different names or varieties of what, for our purposes, are essentially the same chile.

LIST OF RECIPES

FEELS
LIKE
HOME

Plaza Miguel Hidalgo in Banámichi with Nuestra Señora de Loreto church in the background. My grandfather was baptized there.

1

WHERE THE WATER TURNS

THE SUN IS HOT ON MY NECK. It feels good. I spent the night in a frigid hotel room in this high-desert town, where the temperature can fall from 70 degrees during the daytime to 30 degrees at night. The morning air is bracing. I'm in Banámichi, a little pueblo in the state of Sonora, Mexico. It's about a five-hour drive southeast of Tucson, where I was born. I am staring across the sparkling-clean plaza at the old church on the corner and thinking about Margarita Redondo Ronstadt, my great-grandmother.

She would have gone to Mass in that church, and there is where she would have baptized my grandfather. I feel a prickle of tears and a wave of compassion for her. She came to this village as a young bride, married to a widower with four children who was more than thirty years her senior and whose first language was German. When they married, in 1866, he was about fifty years old. She was seventeen. He had brought her to her new home, a wagon ride of several days or even weeks from El Ocuca, the prosperous ranch where she had spent her childhood. Here, on the Río Sonora, her married life would begin. He gave her what comforts the fierce desert would allow.

Friedrich Augustus Ronstadt had immigrated to Mexico from Hanover, Germany, in the early 1840s. Because of his experience as an officer in the German military, he joined the Mexican army and became a colonel, serving under the governor of Sonora, General Ignacio Pesqueira, who is credited with having driven supporters of Emperor Maximilian out of the state during the war with the French in the 1860s. After the war, the general returned to Las Delicias, his ranch on the outskirts of Banámichi. My great-grandfather, educated as a mining engineer, went with him and managed his mines and ranches.

A big ranch in those days was like a small city-state. Most of life's necessities were produced there, including saddles, bridles, boots, and other leather goods, as well as earthenware cooking pots, metalwork, woven baskets, rope, twine, and food. All other necessities and luxuries had to be brought far distances by wagon over rough mountain roads. There was no refrigeration, so the local cuisine depended heavily on preserved food. Meats were hung to dry in strips, fruits were canned or dried, vegetables were pickled and stored to be served later with dried beans, corn, chiles, and wheat. This history had an enormous influence on how food there is produced and brought to the table today.

When my great-grandparents left El Ocuca for the frontier, they weren't poor, but they had a challenging life by modern standards. Like everyone else in that place and time, they survived through strength and ingenuity and communal cooperation. My great-grandfather worked in the mines, so he had to travel to where the mines were, all over Sonora and beyond. Sometimes the family went with him, sometimes

Hanging beef to dry is the age-old way to make carne seca. Don't try this at home unless home is as arid as Sonora.

they waited at home. They never lived in any place for very long, and wherever they went, they were roughing it.

My great-grandmother had help. She didn't have to do all the physical labor, but she had to organize it all and keep the family together, and she still took on a lot of the work herself, including most of the cooking, as well as finding the food and solving any household problems that came up. According to an old family story, my great-grandfather once gave his wife a choice between having a finished floor or a ceiling, because he didn't have enough building material for both. She wisely chose the ceiling.

What could life have been like for Margarita, not even out of her teenage years, packing up and moving and keeping house with young children while her husband went out to make his living and serve the country? I'll never really know, but whenever I'm in this part of the world I find myself wondering about her, trying to piece together fragments of her life, searching for scraps of stories and memories shared by my grandparents and parents, letting my imagination fill in the rest. It's like summoning a dream.

Banámichi. Stress the second syllable. Bah-NAH-mee-chee. It's an Opata Indian word meaning "where the water turns." The water is the Río Sonora, the ribbon that meanders through the desert in northern Mexico, down the mountains from an old mining town, Cananea, greening what it touches, the fields of alfalfa and chiles and wheat and grasses that sprout and bloom amid the mesquite and cactus.

The river connects a chain of villages with ancient names—Bacoachi, Chinapa, Arizpe, Sinoquipe, Banámichi, Huépac—before it turns westward again below Sonora's capital city, Hermosillo, petering out in a series of dams and irrigation canals, always flowing toward but never reaching the Sea of Cortés.

The Río Sonora region is one of the prettiest corners of Mexico, a landscape etched by sunlight and carved by wind and softened by lush evergreens. This stretch of desert happens to be my foothold in the world. I believe in genetic memory, that sense of a place that lives in the bloodstream and passes down the generations. Wherever I've lived, wherever I travel, my soul is always winging it down the road, south over the border, back to my land and my roots in Sonora. I feel the pull from Banámichi like a summons from my father's parents and their parents and grandparents, from a chain of ancestors, most of whom I never knew.

I have a photograph of my great-grandmother taken when she was a young woman. It's a formal portrait, possibly made in a studio or at the family home in Altar, to which the family had recently returned after living on the coast in Guaymas, where her husband's work had taken him. She is wearing a dark floor-length gown and looking rather severe; her hair is gathered back behind her ears, and her right arm rests on a piece of furniture at elbow height.

She gazes out beyond the frame with a solemn look. Though she is young and pretty, there is an emptiness or sadness to her gaze that you can pick up even if you did not know that she had lost a baby, Joe, who died of a respiratory infection. When Joe got sick, she was pregnant, a few days away from having another baby, and they had been traveling a long distance by wagon.

My grandfather Fred, a boy at the time, described in his memoir what happened:

> When we finally reached Altar, Joe was a very sick baby. He developed a severe case of croup. There was no doctor in Altar. The nearest one at Caborca, 25 miles away, was an American druggist. My mother sent a man on horseback to bring this man to see the baby. When he came, Joe thought he was my father and caressed the man's face with his little hands. He could only smile. There was nothing that could be done and poor little Joe choked to death that night.
>
> This nearly killed my mother. She was about to give birth to my brother Pepe. Pepe was born the night of Dec. 24, 1879, a few days after the first Joe died.

Margarita lost three children. After Joe was Rodolfo, who was five when he died of diphtheria, and then there was three-year-old Armando, who died horribly when scalding milk fell onto him from a kitchen table. That left Emilia, Ricardo, José María, who went by Pepe, and Federico, my grandfather.

My grandfather, known in Tucson as Fred, was a man of few words, but he had a very interesting life and many stories to tell. His memoir, *Borderman*, an account of his youth in Sonora in the late nineteenth century, was published posthumously by the University of New Mexico Press in 1993.

He was reserved, a desert stoic, someone who had seen many hardships and saw no point in getting worked up about them. Here he is explaining how he accidentally shot his friend while they were hunting pigeons: "I had to carry him home. He got well but always limped after that. Some muscle must have been injured."

LEFT: Margarita Redondo Ronstadt, my great-grandmother. RIGHT: My grandfather Fred playing his Martin guitar for his daughter, my aunt Luisa, during a party celebrating his and my grandmother's fiftieth wedding anniversary, in February 1954. He died that December.

I am a daughter of that world, though I grew up in middle-class comfort in twentieth-century Tucson, far removed from any need for desert self-sufficiency. I didn't have to herd sheep and cattle, or build livestock fences from mesquite or make rope from cactus fibers. And yet while I am not one of the nineteenth-century Mexican Ronstadts, I do have this in common with them: I love Sonora and feel rooted when I'm there. And my sense of connection to my ancestors is strengthened by my own vivid sensory memories of Sonoran things they also knew and loved, particularly those involving music and food.

In my memoir *Simple Dreams*, I told how those two basic human needs were satisfied together, wonderfully, by the pachanga, the all-day family picnic that was one of the greatest pleasures of growing up in that part of the world:

> This was a Mexican rancher's most cherished form of entertainment. It was a picnic that took up an entire afternoon and evening and could last until midnight. Preparations would begin in the late afternoon, to avoid the worst heat of the day. A good site was chosen under a grove of cottonwood trees so there would be cool shade and a nice breeze. Someone would build a mesquite fire and grill steaks or pork ribs or whatever the local ranches provided. There would be huge, paper-thin Sonoran wheat tortillas being made by hand and baked on a *comal*, which is a smooth, flat piece of iron laid over the fire. Fragrant coffee beans were roasted over the fire too, then brewed and served with refried beans, white ranch cheese, homemade tamales, roasted corn, nopalitos, *calabasitas*, and a variety of chiles.
>
> Around sunset, someone would uncork a bottle of tequila or the local *bacanora*, and people would start tuning up the guitars. The stars blinked on, and the songs sailed into the night. Mostly in Spanish, they were yearning, beautiful songs of love and desperation and despair. My father would often sing the lead, and then aunts, uncles, cousins, and friends joined in with whatever words they

knew or whatever harmonies they could invent. The music never felt like a performance, it simply ebbed and flowed with the rest of the conversation. We children weren't sent off to bed but would crawl into someone's lap and fall asleep to the comforting sound of family voices singing and murmuring in two languages.

TOP: Cooking and eating outside is the Sonoran way. **BOTTOM:** So is singing and drinking. My brother Mike (left), his son Petie, and Alex Flores (on saxophone) played for a gathering in Banámichi in 2015. The mud-encased contraption behind them is a bacanora still.

My grandfather's book includes many beautiful passages about his boyhood on the family farm in Sonora. He had exquisite recall for the things that made his surroundings seem heavenly. Though the family lived on the frontier in a part of Mexico that was remote, wild, and poor, they managed to make creature comforts come into bloom.

> In front of the house we had six tremendously large ash trees. The tops of these trees were as one and in the shade of these beautiful trees we lived most of the time. The orchard had figs, pears, pomegranates, quinces, dates, and about two acres in grapes. . . . We soon had a vegetable patch with a large variety. I used to get my fill of radishes and carrots. One of the date palms near the house would have large bunches of delicious dates in season and Dick and I would fight to climb up to the bunches and pick the ripe ones.

Elsewhere he writes:

> Adjoining our back yard fence was an orchard with coconut palms and tamarindos, a sweet sour fruit used for making a lemonade-like drink, very refreshing. Also we had in our yard two very large *huamochil* trees. The tree grows as large as an oak and the fruit is a pod about three times as large as a pea pod. The meat is white like that of an apple and very sweet.

Fred was an inventive boy. "I also built a small oven where I used to bake pumpkins. I would cut a hole into the pumpkin, take out all the seeds, put in a broken *panocha*, and when the pumpkin was taken out of the oven and cut in two halves we would fill the halves with milk and eat it all with a spoon." Panocha is raw brown sugar, also known as piloncillo or panela, and is still a staple of the Mexican kitchen.

⁎ ⁎ ⁎

It is amazing that a place so roasted by sunlight and heat can summon life in such variety and abundance. The Sonoran Desert is fierce and forbidding, but it is also wildly, amazingly fertile; Sonoran is not the same as Saharan. In the 1930s, the geographer Carl Sauer wrote of the region: "Perhaps no other area in the New World comes as close to the physical conditions of the Old World Fertile Crescent as does this one."

That doesn't mean living there was easy. The Sonorans had to work hard at survival, diverting water to where it was needed and, when crops along the floodplains were not available, roaming upland and down to hunt and forage over great distances.

The historian Cynthia Radding has written about the ancient Sonorans' habit of sharing what they had when they had it—feasting together when food was plentiful and going hungry together when it was not. The sense of mutual obligation seems to persist today. The photographer Bill Steen tells about visiting a family of farmers on the Río Sonora. He went to admire their lush garlic crop and noticed, near the riverbed, a patch of fava beans, a little large for a family plot but too small to be a market crop. They told Bill they had planted those beans for people in the community to take if they wanted.

The Sonorans' ethic of generosity, Radding writes, perplexed the early Jesuits, whose beliefs about crops involved filling granaries and keeping ledgers and building a market economy. The Jesuit missions did not run on capitalist principles of profit, but they did a lot of trading, sending surplus crops by mule train to mining centers throughout Sonora. In more recent times, capitalist agriculture has prevailed there and everywhere, and it has brought with it today's cheap abundance of things to eat and drink, many of them heavily processed and good at making you fat and sick. It has gotten harder to see market efficiency as a blessing and not a curse.

Vaqueros riding beside the Río Sonora near Banámichi.

For many years small mills along the Río Sonora ground wheat into flour. Then the economy shifted. Sonora's celebrated crop is now mostly grown and milled elsewhere in the state, in large-scale industrial operations that use staggering amounts of fertilizer and water in search of ever-greater output and efficiency. Banámichi's old mill is a ruin. The property is tagged with graffiti and choked with weeds, and some of the weeds have become trees. It's easy to taste the effects of industrialization in the tortillas and bread you get today. Modern commercial flour performs differently from the old-fashioned kind I grew up with. To me it tastes rancid. It's the same with lard from factory-farmed pigs versus that rendered from a healthy, pasture-raised animal. We've paid a heavy price for convenience and mass production and global profits.

Much of the Río Sonora's farmland has been taken over for growing cattle feed, but the river still supports some crops grown by family farmers, like alfalfa and garlic, along with the pecan and quince trees. In a few shady spots by the river, you will find bacanora stills, which are always built near springs or running water.

Self-sufficiency and sustainability can be hard to achieve anywhere, but it is especially challenging in a place where water is so scarce. And yet while rain is infrequent, in certain times of the year it arrives with ferocious power. We learned as kids to be alert for cloudbursts, even distant ones, because of flash floods. Any empty streambed, arroyo, or irrigation ditch could be dry one minute and a deadly wall of rushing water, brush, and boulders the next. That's the desert for you—first it gives you too little, then too much, and it's ready to kill anyone who isn't paying attention.

But living in a harsh climate has its rewards. There's something to be said for the way a land of extreme weather sharpens and stokes emotions in a way blander environments can't. In blazing heat, a well-timed passing cloud or the blessed whisper of a breeze feels like an answered prayer. There's relief and almost drunken delight when summer's unbearable grip is finally broken by the wild monsoons of July and August, or even just when the swamp cooler on the roof kicks in and the heat indoors retreats enough for your thoughts to solidify out of boiled mush. (Swamp coolers are low-tech air conditioners that work through the cooling collision of evaporating water and very dry air. Our swamp cooler used pads made of spongy wood shavings

TOP: The ruins of a flour mill in Huépac. **MIDDLE LEFT:** Humans have farmed the rich floodplains of Sonoran rivers for many centuries. **MIDDLE RIGHT:** Organ-pipe cactus is a Sonoran native that is pollinated by bats, which love its nectar and luscious fruit, called pitahaya. **BOTTOM:** Life-giving rains drench the desert in summer.

A blood-red spill from a copper mine in August 2014 poisoned the entire length of the Río Sonora.

that gave off a wonderfully sweet, fibrous, planty smell when the air flowed through them. I always loved it when my dad put fresh pads in the swamp cooler.)

Ofelia Zepeda, a Tohono O'odham poet and linguistics professor at the University of Arizona, writes beautifully about the acutely water-conscious rhythms and emotions of Sonoran life. (Her volumes of poetry include *Ocean Power* and *When It Rains*.) Even with a cloudless sky, she writes, the women of Sonora could tell when a storm was due. "It smells like wetness," they would say, and the aroma was strong enough to wake some people from sleep. Zepeda, who grew up in Stanfield, a little town among cotton fields between Phoenix and Tucson, has also published a book on O'odham grammar, and her poems in O'odham and English are exquisite and spare, like the desert.

She tells how her mother and grandmother would cook breakfast by kerosene lamplight in the hushed dark before sunrise:

> The women planned their day around the heat and the coolness of
> the summer day. They knew the climate and felt confident in it. . . .
> To the women, my mother, my grandmother, there was beauty in
> all these events, the events of a summer rain, the things that preceded
> the rain and the events afterward. They laughed with joy at all of it.

No large human settlements, not even those of the ancient Sonorans, ever achieved some mystical or perpetual balance with nature, but it's hard not to notice how badly out of whack things have gotten in recent times. Water in the desert tends to be treated like ore, to be extracted from the ground until it's gone. As for mining, it has given many people in Sonora a livelihood, including my Mexican forebears, but that, too, exacts its own terrible cost. In 2014 a mine spill at Cananea made the Río Sonora flow blood-red for weeks. The heavy metals in the water spread sickness through the valley and poisoned the river sediment. There was a lot of hand-wringing afterward, and promises of compensation and reform, but many in the valley fear that little has changed and disaster can happen again.

Mexico has a long history of human-caused misery, and this part of the country is as scarred as anyplace else by old cruelties and violence. Much of it was endured by Native peoples whose existence was upended once the Spaniards arrived. In Mexico as in the United States, you don't have to dig far to find the deep veins of racism, or to observe the acute and often toxic consciousness of social status and caste.

But goodness lives here, too. Banámichi and the rest of the Río Sonora also have an enchanted quality, an atmosphere that has always struck me as unusually peaceable and gracious. I think this has to do with the solidarity that seems to have carried on in the way Mexicans and Indigenous peoples and southern Arizona Anglos have long worked together—side by side, up and down the river, across the desert, heedless of the border, which is a relatively recent political invention. In a punishing environment like this, humans need to cooperate to survive. I saw this with my dad, who worked with ranchers and farmers all over the lower half of Arizona and across Sonora. Decency and square dealing were values he and his customers both prized and shared. I miss him. I wish I could have known more of the people in this world he and I descended from.

I was born in Tucson in 1946 and lived there until I was eighteen. Our family was my mother, Ruth Mary; my father, Gilbert; and their four children: Suzy, Peter, me, and Mike, in that order. There are also many, many aunts and uncles and cousins and nieces and nephews and more distant relatives in Arizona and in Mexican Sonora. I've said that our family tree is more like an anthill, one that extends into two countries.

I have never had a home in Sonora, but I get homesick for it. I feel pride in the connection—more than I do in San Francisco, where I have lived for years, and as much as I do in Tucson, the town I was born and raised in, five hours up the highway from Banámichi and in another country, basically the same Sonoran ground but with extra layers of development and money.

A lot of the southern Arizona I knew in the 1950s and '60s has been knocked down and covered over with blacktop and sprawl and ugly architecture. Time rolls forward in the north in a way that it doesn't along the Río Sonora.

For family and friends and special occasions, I still go home to Tucson when I can. A big family gathering or holiday can get Ronstadts pouring out from all over town. No two of us are exactly alike, but when we get together most of us will be ready to sing and play music and cook and eat.

Whenever I'm back in Tucson, I usually head to the Arizona Inn, a gracious old landmark behind big pink vine-covered stucco walls. But after a day or two, once my hometown and I are reconnected, I get hungry for more. Hungry for wider skies and dustier sunlight, for palo verde blossoming in the arroyos, and for the giant columns of cactuses, saguaro and organ-pipe, ennobling the hillsides. Hungry for the long drive south, rolling down the valleys, watching for hawks and braking for goats.

Spanish explorers mistook Los Pilares de Tetuachi, a natural feature along the Río Sonora, for an undiscovered city.

Early Sonorans survived by farming the river valleys and hunting and foraging in the highlands. They wandered when necessary, and stayed put when they could. Even when crops weren't available, the desert supplied plenty of game, fruits, roots, and seeds.

Also hungry as in hungry: for the flaky, floury tortillas, as big as steering wheels and almost as light as Kleenex. For caldo de queso, Sonoran cheese soup, a glistening broth bright with the heat of chiltepín chiles. And for carne asada, grilled over mesquite, and frijoles con chile and quince jelly and coffee roasted with sugar.

I'll call my friends the Steens, Athena and Bill, who have a place out in Elgin, near the border, and we'll get our cattle-rancher friends Deb and Dennis Moroney, from Cochise County, and maybe some of my cousins or nephews and nieces, and we'll all get rolling. We'll head east and down, crossing the border at Naco, taking the highway to Cananea, and then following the river all the way down to Banámichi.

We will check in to the Hotel la Posada del Rio Sonora, and at some point, when things get quiet, I'll step out the door and walk across the empty street to relax on a bench in Plaza Miguel Hidalgo and think about my great-grandmother.

Sitting here, it's hot as hell. The desert sun in late afternoon hits you hard in the chest and face. The glare whitens and harshens everything. But it's a lovely little plaza any time of day. Citizens sweep away the dust every morning, and mop the sidewalks. The skinny cypresses and sycamores give it a formal look, like an Italian cemetery, but don't give decent shade.

LEFT: Bougainvillea blossoms and painted plaster brighten the streets of Banámichi. RIGHT: Rooftop surveillance.

I believe these adobe ruins, in Las Delicias, are what is left of the house where my grandfather was born.

Some villages hum and bustle. Banámichi is not one of them, especially not in this heat. People are inside or at work, the children at school. The dogs are off sleeping somewhere else. Wait long enough and you'll hear a pickup truck go by or, just as likely, the clip-clop of a horse and rider—this is cowboy country. If you squint and look up you can watch the vultures doing loops above the bell tower of the church across the plaza.

Banámichi is as pretty as ever, but today the adobe house in Las Delicias where my grandfather was born is melting into the ground, with cactus growing inside its roofless walls, and mesquite all around. Whenever I visit there, the trees and underbrush are higher, the walls a little lower. In the desert all things return to the soil eventually, but it can take a while.

If I sit on this bench long enough, I can watch the church bell tower, now blindingly white, redden in the glow of dusk and turn to gold. The sun will set behind it, beyond the river, the crickets will start buzzing, and the moon will come out, then the stars.

RECIPES

❀ ❀ ❀

TAMARIND WATER | AGUA DE TAMARINDO

In his memoir, *Borderman*, Federico José María Ronstadt, my grandfather, wrote about his childhood adventures and family tragedies on the Sonoran frontier, and about the wagon business he built in Tucson. There is a matter-of-fact quality to his writing that is very reserved and businesslike. But when it came to music and food, he wrote with such ardor and vivid details that there is just no denying he was a man who really *loved* music and food. One beverage he mentioned was agua de tamarindo, a familiar refreshment across Mexico. This recipe makes the drink he would have enjoyed as a boy in Sonora more than a century ago. You can find tamarind pods in Asian or Latino markets. They come in boxes and look like extra-large dried-out, dirt-brown pea pods. Tamarind is very sour, so this is where raw brown sugar, piloncillo, comes in.

15 dried tamarind pods

8 cups water, divided

1 small piloncillo (brown sugar cone), grated,

or 1 cup brown sugar, divided

Prepare the tamarind pods by removing the brittle outer shell and as many of the fibrous strings as you can. Bring 4 cups of water to boil in a large pot, then add the peeled tamarind. Reduce the heat to medium-low and simmer for 10 minutes. Remove the pot from the heat and let the pods sit in the cooking water to cool completely.

Using your fingers, separate the hard seeds from the sticky paste while keeping the pods in the pot (and don't throw out the water). Discard the seeds and any remaining strings. Add the tamarind paste and cooking water to a blender with ½ cup grated piloncillo or brown sugar. Blend on high until smooth, then add the rest of the piloncillo or sugar to taste. Press the tamarind mixture through a mesh strainer into a pitcher. Add the remaining 4 cups of water and chill for a few hours, or serve immediately over ice with lime wedges.

SONORAN CHEESE SOUP | CALDO DE QUESO

This soup embodies what I love about Sonoran cooking—it's deliciously simple. Some restaurants in Tucson serve a goopy cheese soup and call it Sonoran; this isn't that.

3 tablespoons vegetable oil

3 medium potatoes, peeled and cubed

1 medium white onion, diced

1 medium tomato, diced

5 green Anaheim chiles (also called New Mexico chiles or California chiles), roasted, peeled, and cut into strips

1 teaspoon salt (or to taste)

6 cups chicken broth (preferably homemade)

1 cup milk

8 ounces queso fresco, cut into small cubes

Salt and pepper to taste

Chiltepín chiles for garnish

In a large Dutch oven or heavy-bottomed soup pot, heat the oil over medium heat. Add the potatoes and onion and cook, stirring, until onion is soft, about 4 minutes. Add the tomato, chiles, and salt, and cook another 5 minutes or so.

Add the broth and simmer until the potatoes are soft, then turn the heat to low and taste again for salt. Slowly add the milk.

To serve, put a few cubes of queso fresco into the bottom of each bowl and pour the soup over them, or you can stir all the cheese into the simmering pot. (The Sonoran home cook Armida says this is the old-fashioned way.) Add salt and pepper to taste and serve hot with warm flour tortillas. Garnish with the chiltepín chiles.

Caldo de queso with flaky tortillas and chiltepín chiles on the side.

SONORAN FLOUR TORTILLAS |
TORTILLAS DE AGUA

Ask a homesick Sonoran what they miss eating and they will tell you about the tortillas—big as bicycle wheels, light as cotton, flaky and tender as fine pastry, and all but nonexistent in other parts of Mexico or north of Tucson. They are a dreamlike memory from the saguaro lands.

The Sonoran tortilla, also called a water tortilla, sobaquera tortilla, or just "big tortilla," is made from nothing much—flour, water, fat, and salt. How these plain components could be so flamboyantly transformed is a glorious mystery. How can something so huge be so delicate? How can something so delicate be so huge? If pizza dough could dream, this is what it would wish to become: thin enough to see through, strong enough to wrap a burrito.

Watching a Sonoran tortilla being made is like witnessing a master sleight-of-hand card trick. No props, no tools, just bare-handed magic. A woman picks up a ball of dough a little bigger than a golf ball. She slaps it back and forth between her palms, fast enough to blur the action, hard enough so the ball flattens a little with each impact. Slap, slap, like a gentle round of applause.

With each slap she turns the dough slightly; each turn stretches it a little. The sphere is now a disc, and it's growing. Now it's a saucer . . . a plate . . . a Frisbee. But it's only just getting started. Now it's big enough to drape over her forearm. She stretches and twists it, using her fingers a little here and there to pull it into a circle, tossing and flapping it back and forth and into the air. The tortilla gets lighter as it gets bigger.

Slap, flap, and turn. Flip, flop, and fly.

Other tortillas get their shape through brute submission. A lump of corn masa gets squashed between the metal discs or wooden slabs of a press. A standard flour tortilla is flattened with a rolling pin. The Sonoran tortilla, on the other hand, is born in the open air, on the fly, across an arm, tossed and stretched all the way from fingertips to shoulder, hence the crude nickname "sobaquera": armpit tortilla.

When the tortilla is big enough, the cook lays it gently across the fire-heated dome of a steel comal, where it bubbles and blisters and stretches in the heat. Her fingers test the edge and give it a quick flip to cook the other side, and then it's done.

Seconds ago the dough was cold rubber. Now it's hot silk. She folds it and adds it to the pile, and then, like the God of Genesis working in clay, picks up another ball of dough.

✳ ✳ ✳

Professor Ofelia Zepeda, a poet and linguist at the University of Arizona who composes in English and her native Tohono O'odham language, wrote a poem, "Hot Tortillas," that gets at the reality of this underappreciated women's work. It tells of a woman who expertly makes batch after batch of perfect tortillas in the summer when it's 115 degrees outside, then goes into another room to cool off when her work is done.

> She sits there in silence.
> Letting her body temperature fall to a normal rate.

The poem ends with the lines:

> Her mind and body release themselves from the focus of the heat.
> Most of us know better than to disturb her.

Even though you may not be able to exactly replicate the silken-bedsheet tortillas of Sonora, it's worth trying this recipe to make smallish ones. They will be good, fresh, and tasty and go beautifully with your breakfast eggs or carne asada (p. 118) and frijoles (pp. 140 and 141).

$^2/_3$ cup lard or vegetable shortening, plus a little extra to grease the tortilla dough

About 4 cups flour, plus a little more for rolling tortillas

1 teaspoon salt

About 1 cup warm water

In a large bowl, soften the lard by beating it a little with a wooden spoon. Add the flour, salt, and water. Mix gently with your hands until everything comes together in a ball and then transfer the dough to a lightly floured surface. Knead until the dough is smooth and supple, adjusting the texture with a little flour or water if you have to. The dough should be manageable and stretchy, not runny, sticky, or wet. Break off pieces of dough the size of golf balls (if you

Sonoran tortillas are just wheat, water, fat, and salt, transformed in the desert air.

want basic ten- or twelve-inch tortillas) or racquetballs (if you are ambitious and confident and want to go bigger). Shape the pieces into balls, then smear a little lard over each one and let them rest for 30 minutes, covered by a kitchen towel or plastic wrap. Heat an ungreased cooking surface—a large cast-iron frying pan or pancake griddle will make a fine comal—and make sure it gets plenty hot.

Now shape the balls into tortillas. It's easiest to start by using a rolling pin on a lightly floured surface. Once you have rolled a disc big enough to drape over the back of your fist, do that and then gently pull and stretch the tortilla with your other hand, working gradually around the edges to make it evenly round, as if you are adjusting a tablecloth. Make like a pizza chef, adjusting your techniques as the tortilla gets bigger, stretching and spreading it with both hands, your splayed fingers, over your knuckles—whatever you need to do to get each one as thin and round and evenly sized as possible.

Lay the tortilla carefully down on the hot pan or griddle. Cook it for a few seconds, until it is speckled lightly brown and the raw spots are gone, then flip and cook it a few seconds more—not too long, or it will be board-stiff. Stack them as you make them, wrapped in a kitchen towel. Serve warm.

To make these tortillas delicate, flaky, and perfectly round—not breaking or distorting them into bizarre amoeba shapes with unsightly arms and legs—requires a level of skill you should have already learned from your mother when you were little. If you didn't, then all you can do is practice, practice. Or you can just not worry too much about the shape because you're going to tear them up anyway.

If, by the end, you've made a dough and triumphantly sprayed flour across the room and are left holding something resembling a tortilla, congratulations. Now imagine doing that three or four dozen times more, in a hot kitchen over a wood-fired comal on a blazing, muggy Sonoran day.

RED CHILE SAUCE |
SALSA DE CHILE COLORADO

This sauce is the basis of many, many recipes in Sonora, including enchiladas (p. 32), tamales, and braised beef and pork. One popular and deliciously simple dish is made by tossing the sauce with cooked vegetables: boiled and sliced potatoes, grilled spring onions, steamed green beans, boiled nopalitos (prickly-pear cactus paddles), or boiled baby fava beans, called habitas.

    Many people in Tucson cook with a brand of red chile sauce that comes in a jar. I never liked it, for the same reasons I dislike jarred salsa and jarred spaghetti sauce. This recipe requires a little more effort than store-bought sauce, but it's worth it.

> 15 dried red Anaheim chiles (also called New Mexico chiles or California chiles)
>
> 2 large garlic cloves
>
> 1 tablespoon dried oregano
>
> 3 tablespoons lard or vegetable oil
>
> 1½ tablespoons flour
>
> Salt to taste

Remove the stems and seeds from the chiles and place in a saucepan with 2 cups of water. Bring to a boil, then lower the heat and simmer for about 10 minutes. Drain the chiles, reserving the cooking water.

    Put the chiles, garlic, oregano, and salt (to taste) in a blender and blend into a smooth purée, adding a little of the cooking water if necessary. Press through a medium-mesh strainer into a bowl to remove any stray chile seeds and bits of skin.

    In a large skillet, heat the lard or oil until it shimmers. Add the flour and stir until thick. Turn the heat to medium-low, carefully add the chile mixture (it may splatter), and cook for about 5 to 10 minutes, stirring constantly to avoid burning. Taste as you cook—the salsa will become sweeter and lose its rawness—and add more salt if necessary.

Red chiles, both dried and ground, add heat and depth to Sonoran cooking.

SONORAN ENCHILADAS | ENCHILADAS SONORENSES

These unusual enchiladas are made with thick homemade corn tortillas. Our friend Armida Contreras from the Río Sonora says they are delicious with hot coffee.

2 cups masa harina

1 teaspoon salt

1¾ cups warm water, divided

1 egg

4 ounces grated Colby cheese (about 1½ cups)

¾ teaspoon baking powder

Flour, for dusting tortillas

1 cup red chile sauce (p. 30)

Vegetable oil or lard

½ cup crumbled queso fresco

5 scallions, finely chopped

1 cup shredded iceberg lettuce

Make the masa: Put the masa harina and salt in a large bowl. Slowly add 1¼ cups of warm water, mixing with your fingers until a dough forms. Add the egg, cheese, and baking powder and mix until the dough is smooth and holds its shape. The masa should be light and moist but not sticky at all. If it's too wet, add a little more masa harina. Cover the bowl with a damp kitchen towel or plastic wrap so the masa doesn't dry out.

Make the tortillas: Pinch off egg-sized balls of masa, dust them lightly with flour, and pat them into discs about ¼-inch thick—thicker than regular corn tortillas, but not as thick as hamburgers. (You can also press them into shape between sheets of waxed paper.) Place the tortillas on a plate and cover with plastic wrap.

Heat the salsa, thinned with ½ cup of water, in a small saucepan and keep warm.

In a heavy skillet, heat 1 inch of oil or lard to 375 degrees. Fry the tortillas carefully until golden, about 5 minutes, turning once. Drain on paper towels.

Dip the tortillas in the chile sauce and place on plates, garnishing with the queso fresco, scallions, and lettuce.

Sonora's enchiladas are deliciously simple, combining chewy heat and cool crunch.

A thoroughly Sonoran scene: Our Lady of Guadalupe, with cowboys. Jose Hernandez (left) and Fidel Madero visited this roadside shrine near Arizpe.

2

DESERT PEOPLE

THE LAND OF MY ANCESTORS was for a long time considered the back end of nowhere. To the colonial authorities in Mexico City in the sixteenth and seventeenth centuries, Sonora was savages and cactuses, the desolate northwest rim of New Spain, a blank slate to occupy with soldiers, missionaries, miners, and cattle. Later the Americans saw it as a wild corner of their western frontier, which they were itching to settle and subdue. They envisioned a land of cowboys and Indians, minus the Indians.

To the Indigenous Sonorans, of course, it was the center of everything, their home and world, in the foothills of the western Sierra Madre mountains and the desert plains and valleys below, among the rivers and streams whose fitful meanderings had etched the stony landscape and made human habitation possible.

As dry and hot as it was, as difficult as it was, the Sonorans had worked out a way of living on their land. It was fertile, despite the daunting climate. To survive meant continually adapting, moving, timing crops by anticipating and manipulating the irregular flow of water. For thousands of years Indigenous peoples did all right, planting, hunting, foraging, trading and warring, coping with droughts and floods, dancing and praying for rain, feasting and starving and surviving. Then the Spanish came. They brought cattle and horses, wheat and grapes, muskets and metal tools, diseases and slavery, and Jesus Christ—and things got complicated.

Speaking of complicated: I say "the Sonorans," but that's shorthand. The Indigenous peoples who lived—who still live—in this corner of the world go by many names. It's a long list of distinct societies and cultures, many closely related by language and other bonds—people who were coexisting in and among fluidly defined territories long before the Spaniards arrived, long before the hybrid identity "Mexican" was invented.

One ancient people who lived in these lands for more than a thousand years, from around the birth of Christ until the 1400s, created villages and ceremonial centers on the northern rim of the Sonoran Desert. Their society disappeared less than a century before the Spanish arrived. They left behind exquisite clay pots and stone tools, rock piles that nurtured the agave plants to be used for food and fiber, and the ruins of vast, sophisticated networks of irrigation canals, called acequias in Spanish. No one knows for sure why they went away, or to where. They are the Hohokam, a word that in the Tohono O'odham language means Those Who Have Gone, or Those Who Vanished.

Tohono O'odham means Desert People. They are believed to be descendants of the Hohokam, and many of them live on former Hohokam lands. The Tohono O'odham Nation's reservation extends across much of southern Arizona and into northern Sonora.

The Spanish called them Papagos, which meant Bean Eaters, for the tepary beans that the desert dwellers grew. The label stuck for centuries, even as it came to be seen as crudely insulting. The O'odham, who like other Indigenous peoples have long fought to reclaim their own identity and voice, rejected and retired "Papago" in the 1980s in favor of their own name. The Tohono O'odham are distinct from the Akimel O'odham, the People of the River, who are also descendants of the Hohokam. They traditionally lived close to the Gila, Salt, and Santa Cruz Rivers and are also called Pimas.

("O'odham" is often mispronounced. Don't say it with hard, percussive consonants or like somebody's distant Irish relative. Say it softly, with a gentle break between the o's: Oh-oh-tahm, or Ah-ah-thum.)

Other peoples in the Sonoran mosaic are the Yoeme and Yoreme, also known as Yaquis and Mayos, whose ancestral lands were along the Río Yaqui and Río Mayo, farther south. To the west, the Cunca'ac people, later called the Seri, live in the flatlands near and beside the Sea of Cortés. All across the Sierra Madre foothills

Juanita Ahil harvesting flower buds from a cholla cactus, as Sonorans have done for centuries. The buds, stripped of their ferocious thorns, are delicious roasted or boiled.

and the mountainous north and east were the various bands of Apaches, who raised livestock, settled in seasonal encampments called rancherías, and traded and raided in both Indigenous villages and Spanish towns and ranches in Sonora.

Countless descendants of these and other groups have survived all that the desert and the centuries could throw at them. The Opatas, once the most numerous of the Indigenous peoples in the region, created towns and irrigated agricultural fields in the heartland of the foothills of the Sierra Madre, across a vast swath of Sonora that the Spanish called the Opatería. But by the twentieth century they had all but disappeared. The social scientist David Yetman, who wrote a book about searching for the missing Opatas, said their presence lives on in the names they gave to villages and towns, and to mountains, streams, and even plants, and in the genealogies that their descendants have begun to research. But something brought their society to the vanishing point. The reason, Yetman says, "remains a puzzle."

There's no puzzle about the invasives in the human ecosystem, the ones who came and stayed and proliferated, upending life in these ancient lands forever. They started arriving from Spain in the 1530s. The infamous conquistador Nuño Beltrán de Guzmán led the way. Guzmán's thirst for power and wealth left a trail of death and destruction so severe that even his superiors thought he had overdone it and violated the king's mandate. He went into the northwest desert looking to grab slaves and precious metals, plundering, murdering, and scattering communities along the way. He got as far as Culiacán in Sinaloa. Later, his nephew Diego de Guzmán led the first Spanish foray north into Sonora. They reached the Río Yaqui, but the Yaquis drove them back. The Yaquis mounted such a forceful defense of their lands and families that they gave the Spaniards an early lesson that some desert people were not to be fucked with.

The Sonorans, in fact, established a habit of rebellion and resistance that allowed many of them to preserve their identities and independence against the forces of erasure. A certain lethal prickliness seemed to come with the territory. The history of Sonora is full of pitched struggles among the colonizers and the colonized, with groups forming shifting coalitions with and against the Spanish and one another,

Cowboys in Sonora have been using these all-terrain vehicles since the sixteenth century.

and for a little while against the French, and, for a long time, pretty much everyone against the Apaches.

The Europeans had their own tribes: the soldiers, merchants, fortune hunters, and priests—the Jesuits and Franciscans. The Jesuits came first, following ancient pathways up the river valleys of Sonora, establishing missions as they went. As part of Spain's empire-building project, they were also aiming for conquest, though not so much by armed force. They were spiritual vaqueros, looking to round up maverick souls scattered widely across the desert and get them converted and corralled—settled in close to the missions, putting down crops and roots.

Not everybody got with the new program of planting wheat, toiling on ranches and in mines, building churches, going to Mass, but many Sonorans did, not always voluntarily. They and their descendants were among those who created Mexico as we know it, a deeply Catholic country grown from Indigenous roots that is (mostly) proud of its complicated past and remembers (certain) evangelizing missionaries with (often guarded) admiration and respect. There's a lot of subtext in those ambivalent parentheticals. We could talk all day about the mixed bag of Mexican history, the evil that shadows the beauty. But if we got into colonialism, racism, elitism, patriarchy, and genocide, we'd be here all night, and this is a little book.

A Yaqui woman making tortillas at a roadside stand in Cócorit, Sonora.

* * *

WAIT A MINUTE, YOUR HOLINESS

When I learned in 2015 that Pope Francis had apologized to Indigenous peoples for the brutal harm done to them by the Catholic Church in colonial times but was also about to canonize the Franciscan missionary Junípero Serra, one of the brutalizers, the dissonance was too much to bear. I like this Pope, so I had to write him. Francis is a Jesuit from Argentina and surely understood, better than the usual old Vatican Italians, the full and awful story of how the Mission Indians suffered under Serra.

Even though the story of Serra's journeys in California does not directly involve the borderlands I'm writing about, I hope you will allow me to slightly and momentarily enlarge the frame of reference to include him here. What happened in Mexico happened in California, too, and all over New Spain. The epic collision of cultures and peoples had effects that were repeated over and over. It was the same zealotry and cruelty, the same resistance and suffering. As a Mexican American currently living in California, and with a distant family connection to the Serra expedition, I felt I needed to say something. I wrote this letter based on historical information I learned from the excellent 2015 book *A Cross of Thorns*, by Elias Castillo.

My dear friend the Reverend Mary Moreno, an Episcopal priest, signed the letter with me. (We didn't hear back.)

August 20, 2015

His Holiness, Pope Francis
Apostolic Palace
00120 Vatican City

Your Holiness,

We would like to thank you for your apology to the Indigenous peoples of the Americas regarding their mistreatment at the hands of the Roman Catholic Church. We were expecting this might also include the brutal treatment of the California Mission Indians under the supervision of Father Junípero Serra.

It has been well documented that the Indians, once baptized, were deprived of their liberty to leave the missions, systematically flogged, shackled, starved, burned with brands, and tortured in the stocks for the most minor offenses. Our concern is this: If the Church moves to canonize Junípero Serra, it would dismiss the hundred years plus of enslavement and genocide endured by the California Indians.

During his time, Serra was considered shockingly overzealous by his peers and associates. He was ordered by King Carlos III and Felipe de Neve, the governor of California, to grant the Indians self-rule and to stop abusing them. He did not comply. In a letter to de Neve, preserved in the Santa Barbara Mission Archives Library, he claimed that the first to evangelize the shores of the Americas, some of them subsequently canonized as saints, followed the practice of whipping and beating the Indians when they didn't carry out the friars' orders. He saw no reason not to follow their example. Governor de Neve did not hide his opinion that the Mission Indians' fate was "worse than that of slaves."

The missions' products supplied the army, settlers, and ships that passed through the California ports, their profits greatly amplified by the slave labor so cruelly coerced from the Indians. Serra's history has been carefully whitewashed over the centuries to present him as a kindly, nurturing figure bringing enlightenment and civilization to the poor, primitive Indians. This patronizing attitude is a revisionist lie. The Indians were perfectly civilized, with a culture well-suited to reap the natural bounty of the California wilderness. The Spaniards, far from home and thus free of the moral constraints of their families and culture, were the barbarians.

Among my ancestors in this area was Lieutenant José Ortega, the pathfinder for the Portolá expedition in 1769, which included Father Serra. Another ancestor was Lieutenant José Darío Argüello, who recorded the testimonies of recaptured Indians who had attempted to escape the cruelty of the missions. Their heartbreaking explanations were written in his own hand and are preserved in the national archives in Mexico City. They include the following:

Tiburcio: He testified that after his wife and daughter had died, on five separate occasions Father Danti ordered him whipped because he was crying. For those reasons he fled.

Liborato: He testified that he had left because his mother, two brothers, and three nephews died, all of hunger. So that he would not also die of hunger, he fled.

Magno: He declared that he had run away because, his son being sick, he took care of him and was therefore unable to go out to work. As a result he was given no ration and his son died of hunger.

We know that many of our revered saints were sinners at some point in their lives, but Serra was brazen and unrepentant. Our concern is that to canonize him would not only be an affront to the California Indians that survive, it would tarnish the images of the saints we cherish.

We implore you to reconsider the canonization of Junípero Serra.

Respectfully,

Linda Ronstadt
Reverend Mary Moreno-Richardson
San Francisco

Two views of Tohono O'odham women harvesting cactus fruit. The lithograph on the right was published in 1857; the photo on the left was taken about a century later.

Among the missionaries in Sonora, the best-loved of the bunch was probably Eusebio Francisco Kino, or Padre Kino, a Jesuit who founded a lot of missions and brought a lot of good things with him in his years of horseback travels up and down what the Spaniards called the Pimería Alta, Upper Pima Land. My uncle Edward, my dad's younger brother, was active for many years in the Southwestern Mission Research Center, which aims to keep the Kino missions and their memories alive. Like my dad, he felt deeply connected to the history of the Sonoran borderlands. Though they were Americans and Tucsonans to the core, they also knew they were part of a much older story.

SAINTS AND ANGELS

San Xavier del Bac is the old Franciscan mission church south of Tucson. It's only ten miles from downtown, but far enough away, beyond the office towers and highway sprawl, that it's easy to imagine how it appeared a century ago, when it stood in the Santa Cruz Valley majestically alone.

It's the whiteness that hits you. San Xavier is a pearl in a shell of dusty scrubland. It seems to supply its own incandescence. The mission glistens in the heat of midday and glows in the golden dawn and sunset. It's milky under a desert moon.

They call it one of the finest examples of Spanish colonial architecture in North America. Tourists go there, but it's also a living Catholic parish on the Tohono O'odham reservation. Many worshipers and pilgrims walk for miles on dirt roads to attend Mass.

The luminous simplicity of San Xavier's white towers and dome leaves you unprepared for the polychrome dazzlement inside. The Baroque nave and sanctuary are astoundingly opulent, showing what miracles can be done with plaster, paint, wood, and eighteenth-century ecstatic energy. The pews are wooden and simple, but almost every other inch of the interior—walls to ceilings to dome—is put to aesthetic work, packed with angels and saints, missionaries and martyrs, wood carvings and frescoes, Gospel scenes and ebulliently colored and sculptured ornamentation, including plaster-cast curtains and columns decked with ropes, braids, arabesques, and seashells, and many, many trompe l'oeil geometric blocks. To look down from the choir loft is to stand at the brink of devotional overload.

Inside the San Xavier del Bac mission, passing creatures find both spiritual solace and shade.

San Xavier is a fine example of desert improvisation, where the desire to mimic a great European cathedral of the Middle Ages runs up against a lack of old-growth oak forests and marble quarries. The mission may sound theatrical and garish, but when you're there, the atmosphere is reverential, almost overpowering.

I left Catholicism behind as a girl, and I don't believe in sky gods, demons, or devils, but I have always felt spiritual solace in San Xavier. I savor its otherworldly splendor.

San Xavier's plaster exterior dates to 1906, but the building is far older. It was begun in 1783 and finished . . . well, never. One of its two towers has a dome and cupola, but the other does not. Its lack of symmetry makes it all the more distinctive. My friend Bob Vint, a Tucson architect, has been guiding the misson's current restoration, which has gone on for years and has some years to go. Bob's work has stressed beauty, durability, restraint, and authenticity, and the results have been stunning. The west tower glows the way it did more than a century ago. In 2021, workers enclosed the east tower in scaffolding and began removing cement-based plaster from a previous renovation. That ill-advised coating was brittle and prone to cracking, and it also trapped moisture, which did a lot of hidden damage. The new plaster, based on an ancient recipe, is a mixture of lime, sand, and prickly-pear cactus mucilage, called "la baba de nopal" in Spanish. It can stretch and shrink without cracking in the extreme temperature swings of the desert, protecting the underlying brick.

When I was making a record in Tucson years ago with Emmylou Harris, I took her to San Xavier. Among the intricately carved and clothed statues of sturdy priests and suffering saints, she noticed a pair of simple painted angels on an arch in the choir loft. She was tickled that they were wearing what looked like gingham skirts, as if they had just dropped down from cowgirl Heaven.

My Sonoran ancestors—Spanish on my great-grandmother's and grandmother's side, plus my German great-grandfather—were not Indigenous and did not have the ancient bonds to the land that the O'odham and other peoples do. Our roots go down hundreds of years, not thousands. When my great-grandfather Friedrich Augustus Ronstadt was an infantry colonel in the National Guard of Sonora, from the 1840s to the 1860s, the territory was still unsettled and violent, and it was a time of civil warfare and Indian massacres and rebellions. To my sorrow, I've learned from his military record that he led troops in several battles during which many Indians were killed and captured.

My great-grandfather lived long enough to see that bloody era fade away. He died in 1889, three years after the surrender of the great Apache leader Geronimo. There are roadside monuments in Arizona marking the date—September 6, 1886—as

This cave, dug out of a hillside in Mexican Nogales, was a jail in the 1880s and a tourist restaurant, the Cavern Cafe, from the 1920s to the 1980s. The cafe owners used to say (wrongly) that Geronimo had been jailed there. I knew it as a cool, dark spot for eating venison, antelope, and sea-turtle soup.

the end of all Indian wars in the United States. Well, hurray, but what the triumphal plaques don't say is that the struggle simply shifted toward subtler and less visible forms of subjugation and violence. Apaches—like the other Indigenous peoples of Sonora—have survived to tell their own stories about their past.

That's another long discussion for a different book, but still, it's interesting to see how history has its never-ending echoes and ripples, how the afflictions of a bygone time live on, plain as day, in ours. Take the divisions of class and caste that the Spanish imposed on desert societies, lining people up on a scale of worth from the lightest skin to the darkest. I first became aware of how that worked as a little girl in Catholic elementary school. I learned that the world looked at my dark-skinned Latina friends and classmates much differently than it looked at me. It bothered me. I realized even then that having white skin and a German surname gave me special privileges.

I recently learned, in amazing detail, how my family first got hold of its privilege and status more than two hundred years ago. For this I can thank Cynthia Radding, a history professor at the University of North Carolina, Chapel Hill, who has extensively studied the Sonoran borderlands, with a focus on the ordinary humans—Native peoples and peasants, ranch hands and mineworkers, the powerless and dispossessed—who are generally written out of history texts. She's my kind of academic.

Her 2005 book, *Landscapes of Power and Identity*, includes a short history of El Ocuca, in northwestern Sonora, where my great-grandmother's family, the Redondos, came to acquire a fine expanse of real estate in 1795. Here's how it happened:

In 1770, a Spanish rancher named Prudencio Salazar and his brothers filed a claim to a large stretch of land between the Altar and Magdalena Rivers. The territory was supposedly empty—nominally public acres that the Spanish called "tierras realengas," royal lands. The Salazars had been grazing cattle on the property and wanted to own it.

The process seems to have been pretty simple. The Salazars declared: "We have established our possession . . . in all this land, by virtue of occupying it with our

Road cuts and pavement have made the rock-strewn Sonoran landscape easier to cross, but no less dramatic.

Tilled fields in Tetuachi, a tiny Río Sonora community near Arizpe.

livestock and building corrals that we use to brand and mark our cattle." Surveys were taken and maps drawn. The brothers' payment to the royal treasury came to a little over 156 pesos, plus 16 pesos tax. For that they got about 150,000 acres.

As Radding writes, nobody seems to have consulted the local Sonorans, for whom the land was a valuable communal resource. It had stream-fed fields for planting and hills with grasslands good for gathering seeds and plants and hunting game. If there weren't that many Native people around, well—conveniently for the Spanish—that population was in steep decline. Many Indigenous people were dead from epidemics and warfare or had resettled near the Catholic missions. The area was largely empty of people because it had been emptied of people. That left a lot of room for cattle.

About twenty years after the Salazars took over El Ocuca for ranch land, part of the property passed through inheritance to siblings Miguel Antonio Velasco and María Guadalupe Velasco. In 1795, María Guadalupe, then a widow, started the process of selling her parcel, about 86,000 acres, to Francisco Xavier Redondo, a merchant from Altar. He paid her 200 pesos, plus an additional 105 pesos in taxes to the royal treasury.

Radding writes: "The Ocuca ranch remained in the hands of the Redondo family until the mid-nineteenth century, when, through marriage, it passed to the ownership of a German immigrant, Frederick Augustus Ronstadt. His descendants remained in Sonora and held Ocuca until the 1880s, when they moved to Tucson, Arizona."

This was the pattern across the province—and the continent, for that matter. Land went from wilderness to communal property to private real estate. Boundaries and borders were fixed, maps were drawn, property was claimed, sold, and inherited. Fortunes were made and passed on. The Hispanic people of Mexico became entitled, in all meanings of that word, while Indians were left holding on to memories and dust.

RECIPES

✳ ✳ ✳

DRIED BEEF | CARNE SECA

Carne seca is a direct connection to an age-old way of desert living. Wide, thin strips of beef, salted and air-dried in the desert sun, become lightweight, rigid sheets that last a long time, no refrigeration needed. Carne seca is a vivid reminder of the way history in the borderlands remains close to the surface—the seventeenth century is still as near as any Food City grocery in Tucson or tienda in Sonora. In rural areas you'll see homemade carne seca hanging on wooden racks like rusty-red laundry. In markets, carne seca is sold in plastic bags, sometimes embedded with dried flaked chiles. It's surprisingly light, like wood bark, and a little goes a long way.

The planks of jerkied meat need to be prepared for cooking. Usually they are placed under a broiler until hot and pliable, then pounded in a mortar until fluffy—a startling metamorphosis if you've not seen it before. Reconstituting carne seca in a mortar or molcajete is tedious, though the chef Rick Bayless says you can get much the same result using a blender.

Prepared carne seca is called machaca and is ready to use. It can be bought in this form, pre-pounded, in lightweight bags of what looks like brown cotton candy. It's very popular for breakfast: Fry some chopped onions, tomatoes, and diced jalapeño peppers in vegetable oil, add a small handful of machaca, and cook on medium heat until the machaca is hot and meaty. Add some beaten eggs, then turn the heat down and cook until you've made a fragrant, delicious scramble. Garnish with cilantro and crumbled cheese, and serve with beans and hot flour tortillas.

DRIED-BEEF STEW | CAZUELA DE MACHACA

8 cups water

2 tablespoons lard or vegetable oil

1 ½ tablespoons flour

2 garlic cloves, minced

1 small white onion, diced

1 medium tomato, diced

2 medium potatoes, peeled and diced

8 ounces machaca

3 green Anaheim chiles (also called New Mexico chiles
or California chiles), roasted, peeled, and cut into strips

½ bunch cilantro, chopped

1 teaspoon salt, or to taste

Bring the water to a boil in a saucepan or pot.
    In a large Dutch oven or heavy-bottomed soup pot, heat the lard or oil over medium-high heat until hot. Add the flour and garlic and toast them carefully, stirring, until golden. Add the onion, tomato, potatoes, machaca, and chile strips.
    Carefully add the boiling water. Stir in the cilantro and let the mixture simmer until the potatoes are tender. Add salt to taste.

CHILTEPÍN SALSA

The chiltepín—tiny, round, and super-hot—is the distinctive chile of Sonora. This is a basic chiltepín salsa. There are many variations.

>   2 pounds tomatoes, cooked and peeled, or 1 28-ounce can of whole tomatoes, or 1 32-ounce can or jar of tomato juice
>
>   10 garlic cloves
>
>   1 teaspoon salt
>
>   2 tablespoons dried oregano
>
>   ¼ teaspoon ground cinnamon
>
>   1 teaspoon ground coriander
>
>   ¼ teaspoon ground cloves
>
>   ½ teaspoon sugar
>
>   ½ cup chiltepín chiles (or to taste)
>
>   2 tablespoons apple cider vinegar

Place all the ingredients in a blender and blend thoroughly. This salsa can be kept in glass or plastic bottles, and it will last two months in the refrigerator.

Chiltepín salsa is homemade heat in a jar.

A portrait of my great-grandmother, Margarita Redondo Ronstadt, taken about 1879, when she was about thirty years old.

3
MARGARITA'S LETTERS

In a box in the library of the Arizona History Museum in Tucson is a handful of letters, protected by plastic sleeves, written in the 1880s by my great-grandmother Margarita Redondo Ronstadt. My uncle Edward saved and donated them to the museum, along with many other Ronstadt family papers. They are all we have left of Margarita in her own voice. The letters, in Spanish, can be very hard to read. Her penmanship is neat but spidery, and her spelling is variable. But her heart practically leaps off these sheets of lined paper. To read them is to gain a little insight into the pain and love and suffering that prevailed in those days. Margarita is a frontier mother come to life, someone we would otherwise know only from old photos, or as a name on a cemetery headstone, and whose thoughts we could only guess at.

I have long ached to know more about my great-grandmother, and these few short letters are a tantalizing glimpse into her mind and heart. I wish I had more to read, but I'm grateful for what I have, and grateful to Carlos Quintero of the Southwest Center at the University of Arizona in Tucson, who made these translations. He had the difficult job of poring over the text, adjusting a little here and there for sense and syntax and smoother comprehension, until—as he put it—the living voice of a Mexican abuela, a grandma, emerged from the faded pages.

Here is a letter written to Margarita's son Federico (my grandfather) in Tucson, when he was fifteen years old and working in his apprenticeship with the Dalton family.

Magdalena, June 24, 1883

Señor Don Federico Ronstadt

My dear Federico,

I am writing you this letter with great pleasure to greet you together with all the family. I am very pleased you got permission to come to visit us. . . . I am very excited waiting for the month of October to have the pleasure of seeing you . . . because it is impossible to go out there, not because your papa wouldn't let me. He would if I told him, but he would have to make a sacrifice and I don't like to be so reckless. I could go alone, but with so many kids, I feel bad leaving them alone, because they are dying to see you, especially Pepe. When you come back you will find Rodolfo walking. He is already crawling; he is so cute. Emilia was sick with a very strange ailment. Don Alejandro said it was indigestion, but thank God she is already fine. Ricardo is more terrible by the day; he is exhausting my life and your father's.

I am sending with your papa five pesos to ask Chona or the girls that they buy me two yards of white satin and the rest for a silk lace around four fingers wide. We are all healthy and send greetings to Conchona, Adolfo, Jesusita and Josefita Dalton and the girls. And your mother sends you her heart.

Margarita R. de Ronstadt

In this heart-wrenching letter, Margarita blames herself for the death of her son Armando, who was about three when he pulled a pot of scalding-hot milk onto himself from a kitchen table. According to my grandfather's memoir, Armando lingered for three days. Another son, five-year-old Rodolfo, had just died of diphtheria. The twin tragedies all but tore the family apart: "When I arrived home, I saw the picture of grief was terrible. My brother Joe, who was about seven years old, was still in bed after a bad case of diphtheria. My father's health was poor and his spirit badly broken up." On top of everything else, the letter reveals the family's dire financial problems. It's hard to imagine how families in those days held up when death, suffering, and ruin were always so close at hand. And the Ronstadts were better off than most.

Magdalena, August 9, 1886

Señor Don Federico Ronstadt

My dear Federico,

From the most profound pain, I found the strength to reply to your letter.

Federico, it has been a month today since my adored Armando passed away, and I don't have anybody to relieve me from so many hours of torment. How many times I would see your papa upset by his ailments and commitments and I would send the little boy to him and everything went away. He was so pleasant and cute that everybody loved him. . . . See how bad I am feeling. I don't know how I got the strength to survive for such a long full month. Death would be for me the best possible relief. He is not the first one I have lost, but with the others God sent them illnesses. . . . It takes a piece of my heart that I made the clumsy mistake of leaving the milk where he could reach for it. This thought will kill me. And after this, Pepe, who has always had a weak heart, has fallen very sick from the shock he suffered when my unfortunate Armando got burned. Dr. Roca has seen him and says that his heart is swollen and beats so hard that you can hear it. I pray and take care of him . . . your dad with his ailments, and he doesn't care for himself as the doctor tells him. . . .

As for the businesses, we are in worse shape than ever. . . . The installment for the house was due the first day of the month and we could not make any payment to Don Adolfo. . . .

That's the reason I have removed the servants, to save in expenses. . . . Perhaps if there had been a cook my little boy would have not got burned. . . .

I would go to Altar to sell the orchard, but Federico doesn't want to; he says that there won't be any buyer, and he cannot manage the expenses for the trip. You can see how sad our situation is. We are very happy that you are coming to see us. . . . Your papa, the boys and myself are always looking forward to seeing you. . . . With you coming we will see how we can save the house. . . . Give my regards to your aunt and all the family and receive the heart of your poor mother, who never forgets about you.

Margarita

I'm not sure what's going on in this letter, but it shows that Margarita wrote to her boy as often as possible, and that things were bad.

Magdalena, July 20, 1889

Señor Federico Ronstadt

Tucson

My dear son,

I got your kind letter from the 14th, which I didn't reply to because I was waiting for you to respond to the one I wrote to you the 16th of this month. I am sorry businesses are so bad there . . . given that in these months there is always activity. I was hoping you could solve all your commitments. . . .

I am desperate to leave, days seem years. . . . They say Enrique is going to move today; I'm not sure if he will give me the house today to clean it to see if I can rent it, because I cannot sell it. . . .

Several people tell me that Ricardo is thinking of coming here. . . . He shouldn't do such a thing because it would make the situation we are in worse. God knows the pain we are going through. . . . I am a handful most of the time, and if he came I would have to set up accommodation aside for him, and where am I going to get the money for the expenses? . . . Your mother sends you her heart.

My grandfather was twenty-one when he got this letter from his mother. His father had died in Tucson five months before, after years of frail health. Besides mildly reproaching her son for not writing to her, Margarita explains some of her money woes. Federico was a young man making his way in Tucson, but having just lost his father, and with his mother struggling in Mexico, he had a lot on his shoulders.

Magdalena, August 10, 1889

Señor Federico Ronstadt

My dear son,

With no letter to reply to, I am writing this one to tell you that I was finally lucky enough to have Don Leopoldo coming, and after lots of work he changed the power of attorney from Licenciado Gabilondo and tomorrow he is going to Altar to arrange the promissory note for Araisa and the ones for Salazar and Pompa. . . . Each of them is for 400 pesos, and he says that will vacate. . . .

I am desperate to leave. . . . It is impossible to sell the house, perhaps later it could be sold. . . . Enrique already vacated it, but he left it in ruins, especially the garden . . . so now I am fixing the most necessary things to rent it. . . .

We can really use those eight pesos each month while we sell it. Don't delay your letters so much, because I cannot be in peace without knowing how you are doing. Tell me if Ricardo is working already and how is your business going. Emilia has been sick with a headache that put her in bed for five days, but she is feeling better now.

Last week I received a letter from Doña Griselda telling me about her commitments and asking me to send her the money from here, and I replied to her that I couldn't because I was very busy and with all my business struggling. . . . Everybody sends their regards to you and Ricardo, and your mother sends you her heart.

Margarita

Magdalena agosto 9 de 1886

Señor Don Federico Ronstadt.

Mi querido Federico.

Con el Dolor mas profundo tomo la pluma
para contestar tu amable cartita
Federico hoi ace un mes que dejo de ex
ecistir mi adorado Armando ya no
tengo quien me quite tantas horas de
tormentos cuantas beces beia a tu papa
afligido por sus emfermedades ó por
su compromisos y le despachaba al
muchachito con el y luego le pasaba
todo estaba tan simpatico y tan
gracioso que todo el mundo lo queria
figurate como estare nose como etenielo
fuersa para sobre bibir le un mes
tan largo la muerte seria para mi
el descanso mejor noes el primero
que se me muere pero los hotros Dios
les a mandado las emfermedades
pero ceste pedaso de mi corason que
yo cometi la torpesa de poner la leche
Donde el la alcansara esta considera
cion me matara. y despues de esto
pepe que siempre ha estado emfermo
del corason del susto que tubo cuando
se quemo mi desgraciado Armando
y despues que murio se a puesto mui malo

Reading these letters again, I think about how lucky I am to have even the briefest glimpse into my great-grandmother's struggles and sorrows and the happiness she knew as a loving wife and mother. When you look at pictures of long-dead relatives you never met, it can be hard to see the living turbulence behind those composed and often somber expressions. I can search their faces and imagine things, and marvel at the resemblances to living relatives, but not much more. All lives have joy and anguish and annoyance and hilarity, but photo portraits don't.

A photo is only shadow and light fixed onto a chemical plate and later reproduced in dots and pixels. But if you have one or two, and can add some words on a few pages, you can start piecing things together. You can try, anyway. Thanks to my grandfather, who saved his mother's letters, I think now I have a little better sense of a woman who lived a full and exciting life in perilous times, brought new lives into the world—into my world—and died at age fifty-three. Today I send her my heart.

The Ronstadts at midcentury, in the golden age of grilled meat. My dad, mom, Peter, Suzy, and I posed awkwardly in the backyard for a magazine photo.

4
MI PUEBLO

THE FIRST TIME I SANG on Johnny Cash's TV variety show, in June of 1969, barefoot in my Betsey Johnson dress and hoop earrings and long, straight hippie hair, I was twenty-two and not exactly famous. Johnny introduced me and helpfully spelled my name for the folks at home—R-O-N-S-T-A-D-T—then asked where I was from.

"Tucson, Arizona."

"That's wonderful country," Johnny said. "I like to go out there jackrabbit hunting."

He asked if I went hunting, too. Being a literal-minded person, I assumed that Johnny and I were now going to talk about rabbits. I started blathering to him about tularemia, a nasty bacterial infection that people sometimes got from contact with sick rabbits and rodents. You have to be careful when you skin 'em, I explained. Not surprisingly, that bit was cut from the show. In the clip you can find on YouTube, Johnny and I quickly drop the subject of rabbits and I get on with singing "I Never Will Marry."

You can take the girl out of the desert, but . . . you know. Tucson was still a bit of a frontier town in 1969, and I wasn't far removed from it back then. I had left home just four years earlier and still hated wearing shoes. I went barefoot and naked till I was about five. When I was little, my grandmother and aunts called me "Apachita," little Apache.

We lived on the north side, outside the city limits, in an adobe house my parents built on land that had been part of my grandfather's property. My grandparents had the house next door—about a hundred yards away through the underbrush. They had five acres and we had five. There was a little path you could walk on to get over to their place. As a five-year-old, I used to walk there by myself to say hi.

For longer trips, like heading down to the soda fountain on Fort Lowell Road, I drove with my friend Dana in a cart pulled by her pony, Little Paint.

This was my world when I was little: more desert than houses, and enough room and freedom for children to roam like range cattle. When you walked out the door, you were in the desert. You could saddle up and ride to the Rillito River and keep going to the mountains if you wanted to. The Santa Catalinas, north of the city, are part of the curtain of mountain peaks that encircles my hometown. Living in Tucson, you get to know the stony skyline by heart, and just a glance toward the Catalinas, the Santa Ritas, Sentinel Peak, the Tucsons, or the Rincons can tell you where in the desert bowl you are. If I can't see mountains, I'm lost.

If you've ever seen the 1963 film *Lilies of the Field*, you have a good sense of what it used to look like. Sidney Poitier played Homer Smith, a traveling handyman who builds a chapel in the desert for some German refugee nuns. The film was shot not far from our house, and it captures the sunbaked openness of southern Arizona at midcentury.

Something else that evokes that time and place hangs on a wall in my house in San Francisco: an oil painting of two colorfully dressed women smiling beside the window of an adobe house at a man passing by. It could be old Mexico, but it looks like the Tucson of my childhood, when you could still find whole neighborhoods of adobes lining dusty dirt roads. A few parts of town still look that way. The house in the painting was a brothel. The piece was painted by Maynard Dixon, the great artist of the Southwest and West. He was a good friend of my parents' and had his home and studio near us. My mother had visited Dixon's studio and admired the painting without realizing what those women were up to. Charmed by her naiveté, he gave it to her.

The Rillito didn't run all year, but when it did, it was wonderful to see. There was a lot of really rich farmland around it. There were still some farms at the back of the river when I was growing up, and there were stables and horse pastures and even a rodeo arena nearby, giving the landscape that horsey, hay-bale aroma that smells to me like home.

So of course there were jackrabbits, and also white-winged doves and quail and lizards and snakes and things that howled in the night.

Back then it was still possible to bag dinner from your back door. White-winged doves used to migrate up from Mexico every spring and summer, in enormous flocks. When they came by—my apologies to the doves, but they're really good to eat—my dad or my brother Peter would shoot a couple dozen in the backyard as they flew over our garden. They didn't have to worry about shooting any neighbors, because the neighbors were too far away.

Hunting was a part of our family culture, but my dad had strict rules about it. His brother Alfred had accidentally gotten his arm shot off with a shotgun when they were kids. We weren't allowed to point even toy guns at anyone. My dad taught us how to use the real ones and clean them and always treat them as if they were loaded. I could shoot a rifle when I was six.

But as I explained to Johnny Cash, though I liked eating game, I could never pull the trigger. I was the one who went into the bushes to get the doves, take them into the house, and pluck and clean them for cooking. You could fit about six doves in a pan to fry with bacon, or olive oil and butter. Mushrooms if you had them. You'd turn them over after a while, and when they were brown and done you'd eat them. They were really good. The breast meat was very tender and juicy. You could eat the drumsticks, but they were pretty small. I remember the wishbone was so tiny.

I wouldn't want to ever do that to any dove again.

Cottonwood and eucalyptus trees shaded our house, and creosote bushes and mesquite trees and cactuses filled out the landscape. When the sun went down and the wind picked up and the desert creatures came out, it became a wilder place. I've always been afraid of the dark. I don't believe in anything until it gets dark, and then I believe in *everything*.

Today if you go to East Prince Road and Jackson Avenue, where our house used to be, you'll be well within Tucson city limits, not far from a Wendy's and a Dollar

General. Instead of lonesome old adobes or a whitewashed chapel full of German nuns, you'll see about three dozen brick-and-stucco houses packed into your basic walled-off Arizona subdivision. Many of the cactuses now live in pots on porches. Like so many other rivers in the region, the Rillito has been mostly pumped dry, its sandy bed now colonized by mesquite and palo verde trees and grass.

There were only three sets of lights in the Catalinas at night when I was growing up: from Hacienda del Sol, Grace Mansion, and the radio towers. There were no houses at all on the other side of the river. Now the Catalina foothills are covered with them.

The mountains haven't changed.

I went back to my old neighborhood not long ago, in early spring. Lawrence and I drove slowly down a side road, past house after house. There wasn't much to see over the high stucco security walls or through the chain-link and wrought-iron fencing. The creosote bushes were blooming, lush and butter-yellow, defying the dryness and heat. I reached out the car window and broke off a creosote sprig. It had tiny blossoms and little waxy green leaves and pea-sized fruit. I crumpled the flowers in my hands and took a sniff. The aroma was fresh, strong and resiny. It's the smell of the desert when it rains.

If you think about how much Arizona changed from the day my grandfather moved to Tucson to when my siblings and I joined him on the scene, your amazement can run in either direction: so much changed in his lifetime, and so much stayed the same.

Federico José María Ronstadt arrived in Tucson in 1882, riding up from Magdalena, Sonora, in a wagon with his father. He was fourteen years old. As he tells the story in *Borderman*, his mother and father had discussed where their son should seek his future—in Philadelphia, learning shipbuilding? Or Mexico City, where a military scholarship awaited him? No, said Margarita Redondo Ronstadt to her battle-hardened husband. She wanted no more soldiers in the family.

My grandfather's carriage shop sold the horseless kind, too. This was the auto sales room in 1913.

They settled on Tucson, where Fred wrote, "Mr. Winnall Dalton and his brother-in-law, Adolfo Vasquez, were operating a carriage shop. The carriage and wagon industry was a major one in those days and my parents decided that I could do well in that line."

Federico lived with the Daltons while training as an apprentice. It was a fateful decision, since he not only learned his trade from Winnall, he also ended up marrying Winnall's daughter Guadalupe. He knew her when she was a baby, and she grew up to be a bookkeeper in Fred's shop, when he was a relatively young widower. Their romance is a story in itself.

LUPE AND FRED: A LOVE STORY

Federico José María Ronstadt, known to everyone as Fred, and to me, much later, as Grandpa, went to Tucson in 1882 as an apprentice to a wagon maker. He started the F. Ronstadt Company, which became F. Ronstadt Hardware, which for a long time was the largest seller of farm equipment, tools, and machinery in southern Arizona.

Fred was a pioneering Tucson business owner and civic leader. As a young man he posed for a portrait with his blacksmith's hammer and apron. Even in his workingman's clothes, he looked dignified and reserved. The photo shows him to be full of confidence and drive, and maybe a little swagger.

But he met his match in Maria Guadalupe Agustina Dalton, who went by Lupe. Lupe was my grandmother.

"Dear Fred," she wrote in 1903, in a letter you can read at the Arizona History Museum. "Pepe handed me your letter yesterday and to be frank with you—it pained me, for I'm sorry for you."

Pepe was Fred's brother. Lupe was twenty-one and a bookkeeper at F. Ronstadt Co. Fred was thirty-five and in love with her, as he told her emphatically in several letters preserved in the museum's Ronstadt Family collection.

In those days, matches of older men and younger women were common. At a distance of 120 years, maybe it's possible to look past what is problematic in Fred's ardor and to focus instead on the severity and dignity of the emotions he channeled with pencil and paper, page after aching page. He lays bare his heart and presents it to Lupe in two cupped hands. He is well-equipped, as someone raised on music, literature, and poetry, to make his case, in both Spanish and English. His eloquence is impressive.

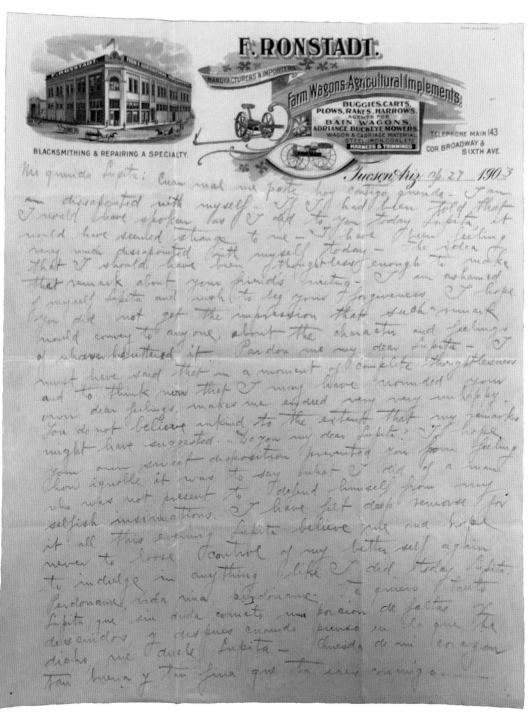

My grandfather poured his heart out to my grandmother, on company stationery, in 1903, a year before they married.

But Lupe's gentle gutsiness in response is perhaps even more so.

The tale is as old as time. Lupe was young and dark-eyed and very pretty. And she was smart, with an excellent command of numbers and a graceful writing style. In a later time, she surely would have had more possible life paths than being a full-time wife and mother. Perhaps she felt no need to settle for the first lonely widower who set his eyes on her.

Fred was a prosperous businessman, well-educated and cultured, who not only built and sold industrial wagons but also played the flute and clarinet in the band he had started, Club Filarmónico Tucsonense, also known around town as the Tucson Philharmonic. He had lost his wife, Sara, to scarlet fever when she was pregnant with their fifth child. Fred knew Lupe's parents well and had known Lupe all her life. She knew he was a good man and maybe was touched by his loneliness.

We don't know all that Lupe was thinking, but we do know what she wrote to Fred:

> It seems hardly possible that I should come to think of you in that way—Friends we've always been and can be truer ones hereafter. I know & feel that any girl has reason to feel proud of receiving your attention. I feel very much so myself, but at the same time I think that I should not under any circumstance lead you to think that I care for you in the way you would have me, for in my heart and way of thinking it would be a crime both against you & myself.

This was Lupe taking control of the situation. She was gentle but firm. Clear-eyed and unapologetic. He was going to have to work for this.

Fred wrote:

My grandfather Federico José María Ronstadt in Tucson in about 1890, when he was twenty-two.

I sometimes see you married to some man you love and who has no conception of the rare gem he has for a life companion. In the vividity of my imagination I can see it clearly and feel like taking him by the throat and strangling him, but when I think of the pain that would give you, I stop the torment of my thoughts and wonder again why it is so in life.

Fred also sent her an acrostic, a style of poem that was popular back then, built from his beloved's name.

L *a luz divina de tus lindos ojos*
U *n mundo de ventura me hace ver*
P *or tí, querida, en mi alma han despertado*
I *luciones dulcicimas sin fin,*
T *u eres del cielo, bien mio, y tus hechizos*
A *mi alma encantan y endulzan a mi ser*

D *e tu pelo dorado la hermosura*

A *me pecho le causa adoracion*

L *os labios dulces y tu frente pura*

T *u linda cabecita y talle angelical*

O *frecen de la gloria tu imagen seductora*

N *i habra en el mundo nunca quien mas inspira amor*

The divine light from your pretty eyes

A world of adventure makes me see

For you, dear, in my soul they have awakened

Endless sweet dreams,

You are from heaven, my dear, and your spells

They enchant my soul and sweeten my being.

From the beauty of your golden hair

It causes me adoration

The sweet lips and your pure brow

Your pretty head and angelic waist

Bring forth from glory your seductive image

There will never be anyone else in the world who inspires
  more love.

In her letter, also on F. Ronstadt stationery, Lupe made it very clear.

I cannot change my heart. It seems I have no control
over it—God alone can do this—I cannot. I do not

want you to feel offended in any way and only ask your pardon if I have hurt you. We are going to be friends— good friends & true ones if we can be nothing else to each other. Trusting you are well and that you will pardon my pencil, I remain
Very sincerely
Lupe Dalton

Fred did not give up. He tried playing it smooth.

Goodnight my dear, dear sweetest of all things in this life to me. Could I but send my soul to you Lupita dearest to say to you how intensely and dearly I love you. I wonder if you are giving me one of your dear sweet thoughts at this very moment?

He tried sulking.

If you would only know how deeply I love you Lupita I believe you could not help liking me a little more than you do.

And he tried pleading. A folded scrap of paper contains this ultimatum, in Spanish and English.

Si quisieras esperar tres meses antes de decidir si realmente mas a tu pretendiente Lupita? En ese tiempo podras conocer tus propios sentimientos.

If you wanted to wait three months before deciding if you really wanted your suitor Lupita? In that time you will be able to know your own feelings.

Will you wait that long Lupita? If you say yes it will make me happy and if in three months you do not care for me, I will not say another word Lupita.

On the same scrap, Lupita writes back:

Not 3 months, but more. It may be that not even then can I say.

Poor Fred. But then something happened. Something in Lupe switched on or off. She reconsidered. Fred closed the deal. How and exactly when this happened is not in any of the museum's letters. The couple were married in 1904, on Valentine's Day. They had a long and loving life together. I remember spending many happy hours in their house, a short walk from mine, enjoying my grandma's cooking and asking my grandpa to tell stories of the old days. I was eight when Grandpa died, in 1954, the year of his and Grandma's fiftieth wedding anniversary. She died in 1974, at ninety-two.

Fred and Lupe had four sons. One was my father, Gilbert, who also grew up to be an affectionate husband and gentle dad. And an enthusiastic suitor. As a student at the University of Arizona, he once rode a horse up the stairs of the Delta Gamma sorority house, looking for a girl who was *not* Ruth Mary Copeman, my mother.

He didn't see Ruth Mary then. But she saw him, and at some point she took matters in hand. They married in 1937.

Fred and Lupe Ronstadt with their four boys (from left): William, Edward, Gilbert, and Alfred.

Grandma and Grandpa were married fifty years, from 1904 to 1954—from Teddy Roosevelt's presidency to "Rock Around the Clock." They had four boys and a family business that grew into a Tucson landmark. My grandfather was known throughout southern Arizona and northern Sonora as a man of great credibility and integrity, and his sons worked hard to live up to his reputation. Grandma was very proper like her husband, but she wasn't stiff. She was warm and loving—there were a lot of grandchildren, but we each had a special relationship with her. She made us all feel like we were the only grandchild she had.

An old photo of the turn-of-the-century Ronstadt wagon shop shows a workplace covered in sawdust, with stacked lumber and a jumble of handsaws, planes, vises, and wagon wheels. A large painted sign hangs high on the wall. It seems to capture something about my no-nonsense grandfather:

TIME IS MONEY. DO NOT TALK TO EMPLOYEES EXCEPT ON BUSINESS. EVERYONE WELCOME.

Not exactly warm, but not unkind. In family photos he always seems somber, holding himself with gentle dignity, in a dress shirt and tie, sitting close beside my grandmother, whom he adored. Perhaps his emotions flared out most fully in his music, a foundation of his life, along with his family and his work. He never had formal conservatory training, but when he was a boy his parents found private instructors for him as they moved between mining towns and when they settled on the family ranch. He learned all he could from them and then took it from there.

Being an amateur didn't stop my grandfather from founding and leading Tucson's first civic band, Club Filarmónico Tucsonense, a military-style unit with brass and woodwinds. He assembled almost two dozen musicians, got their instruments and uniforms, handled the arrangements and orchestrations, composed some pieces, ran the practices, and organized gigs. I imagine he tackled the challenge with the same creative enthusiasm and meticulous attention he gave to building and assembling a sturdy, elegant horse-drawn carriage. It was the age of the community band, and this amateur group of self-made musicians had a fine self-made band-leader. My dad loved *The Music Man*, the musical about a boys' marching band in early 1900s Iowa, because it reminded him of my grandpa. But my grandpa wasn't a con man like Harold Hill, and he really taught his band how to play. They gave weekend concerts in downtown Tucson for years and even did a tour of Southern California in 1896. They had fans across Arizona. The *Arizona Sentinel* reported that when the Philharmonic Club passed through Yuma on the train home from Los Angeles, townspeople and the local band crowded onto the station platform, hoping for an impromptu concert, but the Tucson boys respectfully declined, pleading exhaustion.

These were Grandpa's young adult years, when he was in his first marriage, to Sara Levin. They had four children together. He lost her in 1902, when she died of scarlet fever, pregnant with their fifth child. She was thirty-two. In photos she is lovely, dark-skinned, with a touch of Indian about her, and so young. Her father, Alex Levin, was a prominent Tucson businessman. He owned a brewery and built a beer garden next to it, a lushly planted oasis called Levin's Park. It was an important part of the social life of Tucson in the 1880s, a shady place to escape the heat, drink

Levin's beer and sarsaparilla, and listen to music. My grandfather in his memoir said he went to the "beer park" one night when a small orchestra was playing, and the conductor twisted Fred's arm to fill in on the flute. He stayed and played all night.

Of course he did: Music filled my grandfather's life. He got the love from his parents, nurtured it in Sonora and Tucson, and expressed it richly all his days. It was the same with my grandmother. My grandparents had a book of operatic arias and they could sing and play many of them, along with my aunts and uncles. The itch to make music is a marker that unites generations of Ronstadts. It's one of those stubborn traits we have, like those circus families where everybody from baby to grandma can twist themselves into pretzels and nearly fly. Like lava from a Hawaiian volcano or the oil on Jed Clampett's land, music keeps bubbling out of us.

Not all Ronstadts made a living at it, but music was the homegrown magic we all learned to conjure. I would never say we were unique—most families made music in those do-it-yourself days before radio and recordings, when everyone could sing a little, play a little, and some even compose a little. That's what happens when you are saturated in song from earliest childhood, when melodies and harmonies and chords enter your body through your ears and skin, mingle with your brain cells, and nestle in your heart, the muscle beating a rhythm that keeps you going all your life.

Grandpa passed the musical flame to my aunt Luisa Espinel Ronstadt. She was Fred and Sara's oldest child, born in 1892. She was a singer who performed under the name Luisa Espinel. After beginning a promising opera career, she became intrigued by the folk music of Spain. She studied in San Francisco, New York, Paris, and Madrid, and traveled through Spain, learning its regional folk songs and dances, studying their origins, and collecting a repertoire. To that she added the Mexican songs she had learned from her Sonoran family. She was a scholar, teacher, and researcher, like a Mexican Alan Lomax, but she also sang and danced beautifully, giving recitals across the United States and Latin America.

She brought her show, "Song Pictures of Spain," to high schools, churches, recital halls, and, in 1927, the Edyth Totten Theater in Times Square. ("Señorita Espinel can congratulate herself on a genuine success," said the *New York Times*.) Her aim was to reclaim the beauty and authenticity of traditional Spanish music from stereotypes and caricatures.

In 1946, my aunt Luisa published a book, *Canciones de Mi Padre: Spanish Folksongs from Southern Arizona*. The title page said they were "collected from her father, Don Federico Ronstadt y Redondo." In the late 1980s, I borrowed my aunt Luisa's title and made two records of old Mexican songs from the nineteenth century to the 1940s that I had learned from my own father. I performed them in traditional Mexican dress in a show that toured the country. It was a wonderful experience. Aunt Luisa beat me to it by about fifty years.

Two of my aunt Luisa's publicity photos from the 1920s. She wore exquisite costumes and had the most graceful, delicate hands.

AUNT LUISA'S LETTERS

When my aunt Luisa came to visit, my sister and I were rapt. We thought she was the most exotic creature we'd ever seen. Always impeccably dressed, she had beautiful hands, with liquid fingers that danced when she was fluttering a fan, playing complex rhythms on castanets, and playing the guitar. I wish I could have seen her on stage, singing and dancing traditional songs, dressed in the costumes of the regions where the songs originated. She wore silk and brocade gowns and rebozos, lace mantillas, combs, and piles of jewelry. But I was born too late. At least I have her publicity stills to go by, and her brief comedic appearance as a Gypsy dancer in a 1935 Marlene Dietrich movie, *The Devil Is a Woman.*

I have a photo (p. 5) of my aunt Luisa sitting with my grandfather, listening intently as he plays guitar at home in Tucson in 1954, the year he died. She knew Grandpa far longer than I did, and I am grateful to have been able to learn more about him through her memories.

In 1933 she gave an interview in the form of a letter to the *Arizona Daily Star*. It was a lovingly wistful recollection, expressing emotions that were so familiar to me I could have written the letter myself.

"Childhood is built on beautiful illusions," she wrote about the bittersweet feeling of returning to Tucson and finding that so much had changed.

> Those long summer evenings of my childhood, when the moon made strange patterns on father's guitar as he sang enchanting songs to me, are no more. But the imagination hears the romance and wistfulness of their melodies, hears them with a sweetness as subtle as the fragrance of wild flowers dried in herbs.

She wrote about having to travel "to strange lands in order that I might follow my profession," while holding onto her "many vivid memories of my childhood and of summer vacations spent with my family." Though she and I were a generation apart, we shared much the same Sonoran family story. It's striking how closely my own nostalgia echoes hers:

> I remember the picnics of those summers—our large family—aunts, uncles and cousins—starting before dawn on a large tally-ho bound for Sabino, Oracle, San Xavier and other places. It used to take hours to reach those places then—but after we were settled, the men always went hunting.
>
> Those marvelous picnic breakfasts of rabbit, squab or quail in season; fruits, tortillas, coffee and what not!
>
> Next came the singing. My father always took his guitar on these picnics and would sing for hours to us. Then on the long trips home after twilight we would all sing until we fell asleep with fatigue.
>
> There were other summer evenings I remember when the moon shadows of the grape leaves latticed the arbor and my father sitting there, his face illumined, would accompany his songs on his guitar and later tell us stories of when he was a little boy.
>
> One story always seemed to set him dreaming. He loved his flute, but had little time to practice as the family lived on a ranch, and his work was to assist in the irrigation

projects. In order to practice his flute, he took it with him in the evening and played it while the water slowly oozed around the trees and the peace and stillness of the desert merged with the mystery and enchantment of the night.

The most vivid memories of my childhood are interwoven with music, and mostly the music of my father, who loved it. It was his whole life in those days; his business was a secondary consideration. Being conductor of the Philharmonic band, which used to play in the plaza opposite the old courthouse, he was exceedingly busy. I recall being allowed to attend the long rehearsals with my mother, and when they were over, being too tired and sleepy to walk home, my father used to carry me on his shoulders and tuck me into bed.

Reading this from my aunt Luisa feels like connecting to a visceral cord, a nourishing umbilical that unites me with people I never met or barely knew.

The guitar in that 1954 photo is a Martin, bought brand-new by my grandfather in 1898. It's the same guitar my father gave to me when I left home, with the story of how he got it. When my dad began singing as a young man, his father gave him the guitar and told him, "Ahora que tienes guitarra, nunca tendrás hambre." Now that you own a guitar, you will never be hungry.

Many years later I gave the guitar to my nephew Petie Ronstadt, who plays it and sings with his little daughter, Annabelle. Aunt Luisa had an old guitar, too, one she had bought in Spain in the 1920s. When she died, she left it to my brother Mike, and it gathered dust for about thirty years. At some point Fred Walecki, the owner of a beloved music shop in Los Angeles and an expert in stringed instruments, got a look at it. Fred told Mike that his guitar had been made by the Spanish luthier Antonio de Torres Jurado, who in the 1800s essentially invented the modern classical guitar. Torres guitars are extremely rare and coveted by collectors. Mike sold the guitar and bought a cello for his son Mikey, extending the family musical chain for another generation.

Gilbert Ronstadt, my dad, might have made a living from music, too. He had a lovely baritone, and though he was a quiet, reserved man, he wasn't shy about singing. He performed at the Fox Tucson Theatre downtown in the 1930s as "Gil Ronstadt and His Star-Spangled Megaphone," and he once was offered a job with Paul Whiteman's orchestra, by far the leading dance band of its day. Instead, like George Bailey in *It's a Wonderful Life*, he stayed home and helped run the family business. He and my uncle Edward brought Ronstadt Hardware, successor to the

My dad, Gilbert, also known as Gibby.

carriage company, into the automotive age. My father met and married my mom, Ruth Mary, they raised us four kids, and he led the life of a Tucson businessman and civic leader—and a musician who always sang and played for love, not money. At those all-day family picnics called pachangas, when the guitars came out and the singing started, my dad got most of the attention. People always wanted him to sing. If we were in a restaurant with mariachis, they would come to our table and play and sing, and he'd join in. They were always impressed.

My dad has a professional song credit, for "Lo Siento Mi Vida," which he and I wrote with Kenny Edwards. It's about lost love, mournful in the Mexican way, gentle as it contemplates the arrival of everlasting grief. It was the first song I recorded in Spanish. "I'm sorry, my love," I cry:

La noche que te fuiste	*The night you left*
Cambió mi pobre vida	*My poor life changed*
Quedó mi alma triste	*Sadness filled my soul*
Pensando en mi dolor	*Thinking about my pain*
Cuando brille la luna	*When the moon shines*
Yo sé que no dormirás	*I know you won't sleep*
Ni tú	*Neither you*
Ni yo	*Nor I*
Ya ha llegado el triste pesar	*Sorrow has arrived*
Debemos siempre separarnos.	*We must always be apart.*

The F. Ronstadt Company had humble beginnings, selling what it called "Arizona Bone Dry Wagons."

The family business grew along with Tucson, until it occupied a big part of downtown.

This is the hardware store I knew as a child, with its huge picture windows and all those smartly dressed shoppers in the thriving business district. Today the site is a bus terminal.

The F. Ronstadt Hardware Co. ("Hardware & Industrial Supplies"), where my father spent his working life, was two blocks from the Fox Tucson Theatre, on North Sixth Avenue between Pennington and Congress Streets. It was a gray box covering most of the block: not flashy, but beautiful and exciting to a little girl in the 1950s. With its bold neon signage—TRACTORS MACHINERY HARDWARE HOUSEWARES—and enormous plate-glass windows shaded by awnings, the building was a top-of-the-line downtown American retail establishment. Lots of buildings had awnings on the sidewalks in those days, to make it less brutal to walk around in the midday heat. Everybody dressed up when they went into town. It was a glamorous place for an outing. I loved the luxurious coolness of the stores, with all those shady terrazzo vestibules and air-conditioned interiors, the glistening tile free of desert dust.

Tractors, machinery, hardware, housewares: the store sold all that and more. It had a toy department, which I liked. In the back you could smell the diesel fuel and machine oil. Railroad tracks ran right behind the building so freight cars could bring the heavy machinery in. They would park bulldozers and road graders and other big equipment in the display windows—it was like Macy's for ranchers and construction crews. My siblings and I used to sit on the tractors and watch the people passing by.

We were a classic midcentury family of six. A national magazine did a photo spread on us for a feature about sunbaked Arizona and outdoor grilling. I still have some of the pictures. They are fun to look at, stiffly posed in that campy '50s way. We look like the subjects of a lost documentary called *The Story of Meat*. In one photo, our backyard stone-and-tile grill is covered with steaks as thick as phone books, plus a split chicken. Daddy, in cowboy boots, is placing a charred slab of beef on Mom's plate; you can barely see the plate. Peter and I, in swimsuits, are holding empty plates and waiting our turn. Suzy is looking pretty at the picnic table. Behind her, Grandma and Grandpa sit still as statues in the noonday sun. Grandpa is wearing a tie, of course. Everybody but him is staring at Mom's steak.

My earliest food memory is of meat cooked on the outdoor grill. My brother Peter is like my dad, good at burning meat. All the men in my family can burn meat.

This photo ran with a 1952 article in *The American Magazine*. It called my dad "America's barbecue master," which strikes me as an exaggeration. But he did love charring steaks.

This is a primal desert practice, as the eighteenth-century Jesuit missionary Ignaz Pfefferkorn confirmed in his ethnographic epic, *Sonora: A Description of the Province*: "The Sonoran does not boil meat; that would be too much ceremony for him. It is enough for him if his meat is partly roasted. A thin, pointed piece of wood does him for a spit. On this he sticks the meat, holds it in the flame, turns it around often so that the fire can get at it on all sides, and, after it has sputtered awhile in the fire, it is roasted enough to please him."

Also this: "Hunting is greatly to the liking of the Sonorans. It provides them with their favorite food, meat."

This was the world my mom married into: music and family, sunshine and heat, meat and cigarettes. Ruth Mary Copeman, transplanted from Flint, Michigan, was the gifted math-and-physics-educated daughter of a family marked by brilliance; her father was the prolific inventor Lloyd Copeman. The rubber ice-cube tray and electric stove—those were his, along with dozens of other patents, like a pneumatic grease gun, an automated milking machine, a dripless top for a paint can, an anti-squirrel bird feeder that only small birds could use, and an improved flour sifter. Though my mom was educated at the University of Arizona and had a supple mind fit for unlocking equations, the constraints of her time and place led her down a narrower path. She chose being with my father and making a home. Those old magazine photos include one awkwardly hilarious shot of my mom buying dinner from Mr. Wong, the butcher at R&R Fancy Foods. As he holds up what looks like half a cow for her to inspect, she holds up her hand with thumb and index finger far apart—I want my steaks that thick, Mr. Wong!

My mom had a beautiful relationship with her in-laws. That she was neither Mexican nor Catholic was never a problem. She won them over. She told me she would sit down to a conversation about calculus with my grandfather, who also had an

amazing mind, and he'd leave her behind in three sentences. My mom learned to cook Mexican food from my grandmother, who was a really good cook.

My mother cooked more simply than my grandmother; Ruth Mary was a very Midwestern, meat-and-potatoes kind of cook, but her food was still tasty. Her skill, unusual at the time, was *not* overcooking vegetables. She came from farmers, so she understood freshness. She made perfect broccoli almost every night. Thanks to her, I love broccoli even more than meat.

We always had a garden growing with the desert essentials—corn, squash, and beans—and

Mom and Mr. Wong discussing meat at R&R Fancy Foods.

My mom and dad's engagement photo. They married in 1937.

also snap peas and string beans, tomatoes and asparagus. An irrigation ditch ran down the length of it. We kids had to remember to turn the hose on to keep it filled or the plants would die. The garden kept us fed most of the year. We didn't have to go to the market for lettuce.

I think my parents, like others who went through the Depression and then World War II, with food rationing and victory gardens, ended up being more practical than sentimental about food. My father had his own ideas about living off the land. Once he fried up a white-winged dove that had crashed against our living-room window. "No sense wasting perfectly good meat," he said. Once he shot a javelina, a wild peccary. We'd been taught to eat what we were served, but we didn't think it tasted very good. Actually, it was nasty. People say the desert has such an amazing variety of delicious wild foods, which is true, but not completely. I've eaten snake and hated it. People say it tastes like chicken, but they're wrong. It tastes like snake.

My mother had a broad set of skills, both uncanny and underappreciated. Homemaking was maybe the least of it. She was a wonderful mom, though I think she would have been just as happy to have been a mathematician or forest ranger or meteorologist. She was totally long-suffering with us, because we were always not mowing the lawn and not feeding our horses and not changing the cat box. We were always sitting there singing and playing guitars. My poor mother. Somebody, probably me, left their twelve-string guitar on the sofa, and when she bent over to pick it up, the glue failed on the bridge and the bridge sprang up and smacked her in the face. I heard the crack. I'm yelling, "My guitar!" and my mom's saying, "I've got a black eye."

My mother, so gentle with children, also had a magical way with other critters. She could tame almost anything. Her father was like that, too. Like her, he was very tender-hearted. He'd see horses pulling carts and think they were being badly treated, so he'd rescue them and bring them home, get them fat, and put them out to pasture. It's hard to find a picture of him without an animal in it. It's hard to find an old family picture of any of us without an animal. Everybody's always got ahold of something.

We always had a dog of some kind. We had twenty cats at one point. We had peacocks, like ranchers did in Mexico, because peacocks eat bugs and keep things away with their shrieking, like burglar alarms. They're very protective of their property. My mother once took care of a wild coatimundi, a ring-tailed cat, also called a chulo. She put it in a cage with a turtle, and he turned the turtle on its back and ate it, so my mother got mad and let the chulo go. I had a lamb. My pet rabbit roamed free in the house. I was obsessed with frogs for a while. After summer rainstorms I brought buckets of them into the kitchen, and they left muddy prints all over the floor. My sister had a pig, but my father ate it and she never wanted to speak to him again. We had a donkey. And we had horses.

I love this photo of my dad, who was always a confident rider. I only recently noticed that there's a very short person standing behind that horse. I wish I knew who it was.

LET'S TALK HORSES

The world I'm from has been horse country for five hundred years. I was lucky enough to grow up in a family that was connected to this old Sonoran way of life; you could give our family tree extra branches for all the horses in our lives. (To Murphy, Gilliana, Mischief, Sugar Britches, Blue, Africa, Valentine, Barley Dew, Queenie, Danny Boy, Patsy, Little Paint—hiya! I miss you all.)

When my grandfather was a boy in Sonora, he owned a horse that he had found lying on the ground. It was weak and near death. He gave it water and corn and nurtured it to health. He learned from its brand that it was government property, abandoned by a cavalry troop. Its owner later found out about the rescue and let Grandpa keep it. He remembered it fondly as a good saddle horse, very gentle, "a great pleasure and comfort to me."

The business he built in Tucson was entirely horse-based: wagons and carriages designed to be sturdy and make efficient use of their one or two horsepower. The site of Ronstadt Hardware is now the main bus terminal in downtown Tucson; it's nice to know that the place still helps people get around the city, even if the fuel involved is natural gas and diesel, not oats and hay.

There's a photo of my father as a kid on horseback, wearing the cocky smile of a born horseman. The family legend of his riding a horse up the stairs of a University of Arizona sorority house sounds romantically reckless, not to mention dangerous, but it also sounds like something he would have done. Maybe he couldn't get a car that night and was confident that he could get away with alternative transport: four (legs) on the floor.

Suzy, Peter, and I practically grew up in the saddle. So did Mike, who came along a few years after this photo was taken. My sister and I are on a horse named Gilliana.

You need confidence and skill if you're going to be around horses, if for no other reason than that they weigh half a ton or more. They are prey animals, so they are prone to spook and flinch. They don't have many weapons to fight with, but then neither do we, so if you ever have a fair bare-knuckled and bare-hooved confrontation with a horse, the advantage won't be yours. They can bite, kick, and throw you to the ground, though some are more likely than others to do that. They have personalities that range from sweet to mischievous to homicidal. It's a wonder they tolerate the mean things we do to them. The way we take advantage of animals makes me embarrassed to be a human. Would you enjoy going around all day with a steel bit in the back of your mouth and somebody on top of you smacking your backside? Well, maybe some of you, but not me. And not horses either. The bit is uncomfortable, and aggressive yanking makes it painful.

This is why you approach horses as partners, treat them gently and with respect, and hope they do the same. It always helps to have treats—for me in Tucson it was sweet mesquite beans—so they know you come in peace.

I rode from youngest childhood, from before I can even remember. I was a baby in the saddle holding the pommel, with Suzy holding the reins of a horse named Gilliana. A few years later, when I was about five, my parents got me a pony when I mooned and swooned and swore that I had to have one or die. He was a sometimes-cranky black Shetland named Murphy. I used to bring him into the house so he could escape the summer heat. We'd have ice cream together. When I was six, I got to ride in the rodeo parade, the Fiesta de los Vaqueros, always one of the biggest events and most exciting times of the year in Tucson. Another year that I rode, wearing a Hopi-inspired sunsuit designed by Cele Peterson, my bare midriff and legs got me in trouble with the nuns at school.

Girls of my day were good riders—better than many boys, because of one particular skill only they had to learn. Riding sidesaddle is a strange experience. You're trying to stay on a horse while you're already halfway sliding off it, all because men decided it wasn't ladylike to straddle. But if you're in traditional costume you have no choice, because your skirt and petticoats go down to your ankles, and riding normally would mean you'd have a huge pile of calico and lace mushrooming up into your face. Sidesaddle is the least ridiculous way for a woman dressed like that to ride, which is still not to say that it makes any sense. I will admit that it looks elegant, though.

I have a vivid memory of a near-disaster in a mariachi show when I was in a rodeo arena riding sidesaddle on a horse I didn't know, and who didn't know me. He was a good-looking gelding named Chulo, and he was entirely mellow until some loud feedback in the sound system got him distressed and jumpy. I was singing in Spanish and between lines murmuring in English to Chulo, saying, Please don't kill me, let's get through this together. Everything I said and sang in both languages was heard by the audience. But that horse was a trouper, and I survived and took Chulo home with me.

Sonorans are some of the best riders anywhere; they have close working relationships with their horses, and they form a two-species unit, four legs on the ground, two arms in the air, and two heads working together to get cattle rounded up. Watching Mexican horsemen in a charreada, a rodeo, is a thrill; the agility of their mounts is mesmerizing, the instructions from the rider so subtle and the results so precise. To see smoother footwork you'd have to consult a Fred and Ginger movie.

Americans have been taught to believe that the whole riding-and-roping cowboy thing began in our Wild West, out in Texas or Wyoming or someplace, and then was refined by Gene Autry and Roy Rogers and perfected by John Wayne. It wasn't like that. Cowboying is like surfing and rock-and-roll, something white people picked up in their travels and liked so much they eventually started to think they owned it and must have invented it.

Cowboys are what you get when you raise cattle in wide-open spaces that are too big to fence in and where animals have to roam far and wide to find enough to eat. That is, the deserts, mountains, and canyons of northern Mexico. Getting the herd all back together for one last trip to the slaughterhouse was a job for men on horses. The men who handled the cows, las vacas, were vaqueros. When you call someone "buckaroo," you are mispronouncing "vaquero." When you wear a shirt with a yoke collar and pearl-snap buttons, bell-bottom pants, a Roy Rogers hat to shade your face, hand-stitched boots, and chaps to protect your legs from the thorny brush, you are flashing high-style Sonoran fashion, circa 1820. The same goes with using a Western

TOP: It was fun to ride in the Tucson Rodeo Parade. One year I wore traditional Navajo attire and won a prize. (That's Peter in the foreground.) BOTTOM: I made friends with a palomino on a trip along the Río Sonora in 2013. I tried to pick burrs out of its mane.

saddle, which is smoothly shaped for comfort and for distributing a rider's weight, which helps both you and the horse endure the endless hours of riding fence and chasing cattle.

I could ride, and I liked to dress like a cowboy, but I was never that good at roping. I once recorded an old cowboy song, "Old Paint," that we all sang together as kids growing up. For a long time I didn't understand all the words: "I ride an old paint / I lead an old dam / I'm going to Montana / to throw a houlihan."

What the heck is a houlihan, I thought. After years of wondering, I finally asked my friend Deb Moroney, who is a real cowgirl in Cochise County, in addition to being a medical doctor. (She and her husband, Dennis, raise Criollo cattle, a rugged, desert-hardened breed descended from the original livestock brought by the Spaniards centuries ago.) Deb showed me that a houlihan is an overhead throw of a lariat, a way to rope a horse or calf around the neck. You start by holding the lariat loop down at your side while you approach your target. Then, instead of whirling the loop overhead, you swing it forward and back a few times, to build momentum. Finally, with a quick overhand flick of the arm, you let fly—ideally with just one swing, so you don't spook the animal. It's a basic vaquero move that is second nature to someone like Deb.

In my family, the two oldest kids, Suzy and Peter, were really close. I was seven years younger than Suzy and five years younger than Peter, so I was the tagalong. But once I could sing the high harmonies, I became necessary. Mike arrived in 1953 and joined the family chorus not long after.

It's hard to express how much we kids owed to our mom, dad, and Ronstadt grandparents for the world of music we grew up in. The songs they gave us were the richest inheritance any children could hope for, and we started collecting it from the cradle. There were our father's haunting lullabies, like "Canto de Cuña," about the coyote in the sky with eyes of silver and feet of mercury, and the wickedly funny songs our mom taught us, like the one about a mother being torn apart by lions, and about the baby who died to spite us, of spinal meningitis. We were forever singing with one another around the house—Suzy was crazy for Hank Williams—or harmonizing on Mexican tunes with our dad in the car, or listening with our grandparents to old opera 78s and to Saturday broadcasts of the Metropolitan Opera.

Suzy had the stamina and skills of a classic Sonoran housewife and mother, which she later put to use raising her own blended family of eight kids. She knew how to do everything. She could fix the roof, repair a pump, doctor a horse, take care of the kids, and every day get three delicious meals on the table. She was a great cook.

She had a lovely, pure alto voice, which blended beautifully with Peter's and mine when we sang together in a folk trio called the New Union Ramblers. We played in clubs around town, and sometimes at the dress store downtown owned by Cele Peterson, my friend Katya's mother. Cele liked to support local talent, so she had us sing for the shoppers at her 6 a.m. early-bird sale. Ladies would be fighting over dresses while we were in the corner blaring an old Jim Reeves tune we had learned somewhere: "Railroad, steamboat, river, and canal. Yonder comes a sucker and he's got my gal."

In our trio, Suzy always sang lead on "I Never Will Marry," but then she married, so I took it over. According to Ronstadt family rules, if you sing the song first, it's yours forever, unless there is some really good reason to switch. "Over the Rainbow" belonged to Peter, because he sang it first as a soprano in the Tucson Arizona Boys

Chorus. Then his voice changed and I got it. He and I used to sing "Over the Rainbow" in four-part harmony with our cousins Johnny and Bill.

Peter's musical ability bloomed very early. He was a standout member of the boys' chorus, a widely respected group that toured the country and the world. He was a soloist whose otherworldly soprano gave audiences chills in concerts at the old Temple of Music and Art downtown, where my aunt Luisa once performed. In high school Peter had a rock-and-roll band, the Nightbeats. They had a hit record in Australia, "Doreen."

Peter eventually put aside his longish hair and guitar for a gun and a badge. He became a city cop and then the top cop, working as Tucson's police chief in the 1980s. He was greatly admired by his officers. Peter has always been my straight-arrow older brother, the former fraternity boy with the master's degree in government and Latin American history from the University of Arizona. He also studied at the FBI Academy. With his enviably fluent Spanish, he navigated the Anglo and Mexican worlds of Tucson with ease and great skill.

Peter was the best harmony singer in our family group. He has an uncanny ear for it. Though he was always a by-the-books cop, he has a gentle heart that warms to the sentiments and sorrows of old Mexican music. We used to fight ferociously as rival siblings, but he always knows how to make me laugh, and his wife, Jackie, is a peach. We call her Big Jackie to avoid confusion with my nephew Petie's wife, Little Jackie.

Our younger brother, Mike, was so important in keeping the Ronstadt musical flame alive—and for a while the family business, too. He ran what was left of the hardware store after the big-box stores forced Ronstadt Hardware to shut down. Mike was probably the smartest of the four of us. He had my mother's love for science and math, and my father's ability to fix anything.

He was also a gifted musician and songwriter. My favorite song of his is "Canadian Moon," which tells how much the desert can haunt you with homesickness even when you are luxuriating in the cool northern green of the Canadian West. Mike sang in a trio with our cousins Bill and John. Later, he played in a band with his two sons: Mikey, who plays the cello, and Petie, who plays everything else.

Mike always had a beard, and whether it was black or gray, it always made people mistake him for the best-known Doobie Brother. For years he signed autographs as "Michael McDonald" because he figured giving eager fans what they wanted was quicker and easier than explaining who he really was and disappointing them. People would come up and shyly ask, "Is your name Michael?" And he'd say, "Sure!" and sign. (I will confess here that I sometimes signed my name "Sally Field," back when Sally was Sister Bertrille, the Flying Nun. Except for the white habit and wimple, Sally and I looked a lot alike, with our bangs and chubby cheeks.)

For years Mike had a family band, Ronstadt Generations, with his sons, Mikey and Petie, that recorded and toured far and wide, performing traditional and original songs of the Southwest and old family songs from Mexico. The jobs and marriages sometimes changed and the kids grew up, but we all kept singing, especially at family gatherings and holidays, savoring every chance we got.

I visited Peter not long ago, and we sat and talked for a couple of hours about old times, trying to close the gaps in our recollections and correcting each other and basically being old together. He told me some stories I had never heard before, and I shook loose some memories he'd forgotten. But the minute somebody mentioned—and we started singing—the old western song "Ragtime Cowboy Joe," that highfalutin' rootin' tootin' son of a gun from Arizona popped immediately out of the deep childhood part of our brains. Peter and I used to sing it in three-part harmony with Suzy.

When I was downtown and done visiting the hardware store as a kid, I'd sometimes walk the few blocks to Cele Peterson's dress shop, press my nose against the window, and drool over the beautiful evening gowns she had on display. I could only dream of owning one.

Cele was one of the most important business owners in Tucson, but when I was a girl I knew her as a friend of my mom's, and as the mother of Katya. Katya

Cele Peterson looking gorgeous in one of her designs. She made stylish, practical clothes for desert dwellers.

and I grew up together, and she remains one of my closest friends. Cele's shop carried designer clothing from New York and European houses, as well as her own creations. Her designs were perfect for the Southwest, made of practical fabrics like lightweight denim, mattress ticking, and bandanna cloth. The elegant finishing often included handmade sterling-silver buttons.

Cele was best known for gowns and glamour, and Mexican women who could afford it crossed the border regularly to shop in her store. Her business was an important social and economic bridge between Tucson and northern Mexico.

Cele was beautiful, with alabaster skin and wavy black hair that hung nearly to her waist. She collected her hair into a chignon that she secured with two sterling-silver combs. A sterling cuff bracelet on each wrist and a choker of good pearls were all she needed to look stunning, regardless of whatever else she was wearing, and I never saw her dressed any other way. She knew the difference between style and fashion, and she had style. She retained that style from her twenties until her death at age 101. She never looked dated.

Cele grew up in Bisbee, a copper-mining town southeast of Tucson. She claimed to have met Wyatt Earp, and as a young child she used to climb up a tall hill to gaze over the border at some of the late bloody skirmishes of the Mexican civil war. She moved to Tucson, married, and, during the Great Depression, opened a dress shop, which succeeded despite the stagnant economy. She often traveled for business, and I once asked her if she had ever been afraid of being a woman traveling alone. She replied that if anyone ever crossed her boundary, she would open her handbag and show him the little gun that she always carried there. I was shocked.

When downtown shopping died, partly because of the crash of the Mexican peso and the rise of suburban shopping malls, an important economic link to Mexico was severed. My father's business was among many that didn't survive, but Cele was able to reopen in suburbia. Being out of downtown didn't have the same cozy sense of community, but once you were inside the store, Cele made you feel at home. She continued dealing with loyal customers in English or Spanish well into the 2000s, and she knew everything that was going on in town and who was doing it. Cele knew where all the bodies were buried and what size they wore.

Cele and my mom once took five of us kids—Katya and her sister Quinta, their brother Pancho, and me and my little brother, Mike—on a summer road trip to Guadalajara. We went down in Cele's Cadillac, with my mother at the wheel. I was twelve. It felt glamorous and grown-up, shopping and relaxing and exploring the city. I remember the roses and jacarandas were in bloom and the breezes carried the scent of roses everywhere. Because we were chaperoned, Katya, Pancho, and I could socialize with older kids and go to their parties. I was serenaded twice on that trip, and one of the guys later asked me to marry him. His name was Mario. He was seventeen. He brought a whole mariachi band with him for the serenade; they showed up in two taxis. He later sent in the mail a pin from his military school, an acrostic word puzzle made from my name (like the one my grandfather sent to my grandmother in 1903), and a marriage proposal. I knew he wasn't making plans to wed a twelve-year-old anytime soon; he was just putting his marker down, as young men of that day did. I was making plans to enter eighth grade. I refused him, as politely as I could.

Marriage was one Ronstadt family occupation I did not pursue. There were plenty of other Ronstadts to pick up the slack, and those who married and raised families could be very prolific. One uncle and aunt had twelve children, and the others each had about two to four. There was a Ronstadt behind every blade of grass, and a lot of them went to Catholic school. The same nun who had taught my dad and older

Suzy, Peter, and I dressed up for a concert by flamenco dancer José Greco at the Temple of Music and Art in Tucson.

siblings at Saints Peter & Paul taught me. Her name was Sister Francis Mary, and when I had her in second grade, she was one thousand years old. We loved Sister Francis Mary, but she did not mellow with age.

The sisters wanted you to speak English. If you spoke Spanish in the classroom or the schoolyard, you were punished. I didn't speak Spanish, so it wasn't a problem for me. Peter is the only one of us kids who really became fluent in the language. Suzy could hold her own, and Mike could get along in Spanish in the present tense, but I'm just hopeless. My first words were in Spanish, but it didn't stick, and school was no help. For me, Spanish was the language you got scolded and praised in, and the language you sang in. Since I always sang in Spanish, it was always more natural for me to sing it than speak it.

You might ask why a place as indelibly Mexican as Tucson would punish schoolchildren for speaking the local language. Or how members of a family like mine would mostly lose the mother tongue after my father's generation. The Tucson of my early childhood was segregated, both by law and by hardened practice. The divisions by color, race, and class, though not always talked about, were sharply drawn. While Mexicans and Indians did not endure the same kind of forced segregation that Black Americans did in those Jim Crow days, they occupied a world apart from Anglo Tucson. Mexicans mostly lived south and west of downtown, along with many Black and Chinese American families. Anglos lived north and east. The groups were separated, literally, by railroad tracks.

Whether public or parochial, the schools wanted to Americanize the brown kids and drive their culture out of them. The city fathers wanted Tucson to be a great twentieth-century boomtown, to fit Anglo ideas of modernity and progress. Over the years this meant changing street names from Spanish to English, building freeways that separated and isolated neighborhoods, and ultimately bulldozing historic parts of town in the name of urban renewal and "slum" clearance. In her poignant 2010 book, *La Calle*, historian Lydia Otero tells how eighty acres of the most densely populated blocks in all of Arizona were leveled in the 1960s, and the poor folks pushed farther south. New civic buildings and parking lots went up in place of old adobe homes that once opened right onto the street, where Mexican, Black, and Chinese families and merchants had lived and worked for generations. Among other things, the government built a community center that destroyed a community.

Though my grandparents were staunchly Mexican and my father and his brothers were equally proud of their roots, the Ronstadts were not working-class or poor and therefore had more of a choice over where to live and what social circles to move in. We lived on the north side of town, far from the barrio.

Of course I was barely aware of these things as a shy little girl adjusting to life in the first grade. Growing up in the bubble of white privilege, with a German surname, shielded me from a lot of grief. But I soon learned about the rules of color and caste in the little whispered references about skin color—which girls were dark, and who was particularly dark.

My friend Patsy and her siblings were very well-liked, but they faced hurdles I never had to deal with. Patsy told me a childhood story about the old El Conquistador Hotel on East Broadway, which opened its swimming pool in summer to local residents for a small fee. She and her sisters went there one day with her brother-in-law. "The lifeguard told him, 'We don't allow Blacks.' When John told him we were with him and were Mexican, he made us all get out, because 'dark people' weren't allowed to swim with whites." The hotel was demolished long ago. I've heard similar stories about the city-owned pool in Oury Park, which allowed Black and brown people to swim only one day a week—the day before they closed the pool to clean it.

The Ronstadts had land and a major downtown business, and Don Federico was a pillar of the community. We weren't fully white, but we were white enough, and the white society took us in. My parents never really talked about it when we were kids, but later my mom told me that my dad would be at a cocktail party and, after three rounds of drinks, people would start talking about those dirty Mexicans. And my dad would say: "You can't talk like that here." People didn't argue with my dad too much. He had a real presence. He wasn't menacing or threatening, he was just very there. On his feet.

Lalo Guerrero, the father of Chicano music, circa 1948.

South of downtown, east of the freeway and the Santa Cruz River, there are still some old adobe homes in the blocks around Meyer Street, once the commercial heart of Mexican-American Tucson. Money managers and lawyers and people in media live in them now, paying architects tons of money to repair the stucco and install tasteful antique light fixtures to evoke the bygone days.

The great Chicano musician and songwriter Lalo Guerrero grew up on Meyer in the old barrio. Lalo wrote lots of hits from the 1940s through the '60s—beautiful love songs and novelty tunes like "Pancho Claus" and "There's No Tortillas," which reworks "O Sole Mio" to express a Mexican's operatic despair when he realizes there's only bread. (I know the feeling.) Lalo was a great bandleader and Mexican American activist, a defender of farmworkers' and women's rights. He was a good friend of my dad's, and they sang together often. The two of them serenaded me at my bedroom door on my third birthday. They asked what song I wanted to hear, and I told them "La Burrita," about a little donkey going to market.

Lalo lived in Los Angeles and Palm Springs, but he kept his hometown and his Tucson family close to his heart. He was always so hip—I remember seeing him in a Tucson parade wearing a new zoot suit with a long chain, looking as suave as he had as a young man. Lalo sang and played long enough to be recognized as a national treasure. He received the National Medal of Arts from President Bill Clinton in 1996 and kept on working. He was writing and recording at the top of his talent, and with top musicians like Ry Cooder and Los Lobos, until very late in his life.

In the 1990s he wrote "Barrio Viejo," a lament for his vanished community. The version he sang on Ry's album *Chávez Ravine*, in 2005, can tear your heart to bits.

Viejo barrio, Barrio Viejo.

Solo hay lugares parejos.

Donde un día hubo casas,

Donde vivió nuestra raza.

Solo quedan los escombros,

De los hogares felices,

De las alegres familias,

De esa gente que yo quisé.

Por las tardes se sentaban,

Afuera a tomar el fresco.

Yo pasaba y saludaba,

Ya parece oigo el eco.

¿Cómo está, Doña Juanita?

Buenas tardes, Isabel.

¿Hola que dices, Chalita?

¿Como está Arturo y Manuel?

Viejo barrio, Barrio Viejo.

Que en mi infancia te gocé.

Y con todos mis amigos,

Iba descalzo y a pie.

De la Meyer hasta El Hoyo,

Desde El Hoyo hasta la acequia,

De la acequia hasta el río,

Ese era el mundo mio.

The old neighborhood, Barrio Viejo.

What remains all looks the same.

When at one time there were houses,

Where our people lived.

All that's left are fragments,

Of those happy homes,

Of joyous families,

Of the people that I loved.

They would sit in the afternoon,

Outside to take in fresh air.

I would pass by and greet them,

I can almost hear the echo.

How've you been, Juanita?

Good afternoon, Isabel.

What do you say, Chalita?

How are Arturo and Manuel?

The old neighborhood, Barrio Viejo.

That I enjoyed as a child.

And with my friends,

Walking barefoot we went.

From Meyer to El Hoyo,

From El Hoyo to the canal,

From the canal to the river,

That was my world.

Dicen que éramos pobres,
Pues yo nunca lo noté.
Yo era feliz en mi mundo,
De aquel barrio que adoré.

Bonitas las serenatas,
A las tres de la mañana,
Que le cantaba a mi chata,
Pegadita a su ventana.

Por la calle del Convento,
Una casa destruida,
Quedó como monumento
Al gran amor de mi vida.

Pobrecito viejo barrio.
Como te debe doler,
Cuando en nombre del progreso,
Derrumban otra pared.

Viejo barrio, Barrio Viejo.
Yo también ya envejecí.
Y cuando uno se hace viejo,
Nadie se acuerda de ti.

Vámonos muriendo juntos.
Que me entierren en tu suelo.
Y seremos dos difuntos,
Rodeados de mil recuerdos.

They say that we were poor,
But I never noticed.
I was happy in my world,
Of that neighborhood that I adored.

The serenades were lovely,
At three in the morning,
That I sang to my sweetheart,
Right next to her window.

On Convent Street,
A ruined house,
Remained as a monument
To the great love of my life.

Poor old neighborhood.
How it must hurt you,
When in the name of progress,
They tear down another wall.

The old neighborhood, Barrio Viejo.
I too have grown old.
And when you get old,
Nobody remembers you.

Let us die together.
May they bury me in your soil.
And we'll be two departed ones,
Surrounded by a thousand memories.

Lalo sang this song in his last public appearance before he died. In the liner notes for *Chavez Ravine*, a record dedicated to the destruction of another beloved Mexican neighborhood, this one in Los Angeles, Ry wrote: "Emotion and memory remain long after the maps are rolled up and put away and the black-and-white photographs are boxed up and taken down to the basement." He added: "I think Lalo's homage to his old barrio will probably outlive all the venues of power, but, sadly, not Lalo himself. He passed into the legend of history on March 17, 2005. Viva El Chicano Inolvidable."

Long Live the Unforgettable Chicano.

RECIPES

✻ ✻ ✻

GRILLED STEAK | CARNE ASADA

This Sonoran classic is utterly simple, but when done right, it becomes the heart of a meal you won't forget. The meat is seasoned only with salt, then grilled quickly over very hot coals until charred outside and juicy inside.

Prepare a bed of charcoal, preferably mesquite. Make it so hot you can hold your hand over it for only a few seconds. Season the grill by rubbing it with fat: Use tongs to hold a tightly rolled-up paper towel dipped in vegetable oil, or to rub the grill with beef fat trimmed from your steaks.

Grill the steaks. Use top-quality meat: skirt steaks or other steaks, sirloin or chuck, sliced or pounded to ¼-inch or ½-inch thickness. Diezmillo, or chuck roll, is a traditional cut used in Sonora. Sprinkle the steaks with sea salt just before or after placing them on the grill. Cook the steaks until you see bloody juices gathering on top and grill marks on the bottom, about 2 to 4 minutes per side, turning just once. Aim for medium, not medium-rare.

Let the grilled steaks rest in a covered platter or bowl, then slice or roughly chop for serving. While you're cooking the meat, grill some spring onions, too, until charred and tender.

Assemble the feast: grilled steaks and onions piled into soft flour tortillas smeared with frijoles de la olla (p. 139), with guacamole and salsa (p. 119) on the side, salt for sprinkling, and lime wedges to squeeze over everything, including your cold Tecate beers. Add music and serve.

Luz Corrales and her son Beto Corella grilling carne asada and spring onions at a festival in the little Río Sonora town of Baviácora.

GREEN CHILE AND TOMATO SALSA | SALSA DE CHILE VERDE CON TOMATE

This salsa is good with carne asada (p. 118).

> 6 green Anaheim chiles (also called New Mexico chiles or California chiles)
>
> 3 large tomatoes
>
> 1 bunch cilantro, finely chopped
>
> 1 teaspoon salt
>
> 1 teaspoon pepper

To roast the chiles, hold them with tongs over a gas burner, or put them on a sheet pan under a broiler or on an outdoor grill. Turn them as they roast, until they are almost completely blackened. Be thorough, but don't go overboard; you don't want the chiles to be dried out and crispy, but if you leave too many waxy green areas, they will be very hard to peel. Place the blackened chiles in a paper or plastic bag and close tightly, or cover the chiles with a damp kitchen towel. Let the chiles cool, then remove their skins, stems, and seeds. Cut the chiles into ½-inch strips, then coarsely chop.

Bring a pot of water to boil for the tomatoes. Make shallow cuts in the tomatoes to make them easier to peel, then boil them for about 2 minutes. Remove the tomatoes from the pot (do not discard the water), let them cool slightly, and then peel them. Return the peeled tomatoes to their cooking water until the salsa is finished.

Put the tomatoes in a large bowl and mash them lightly, then add the roasted chiles, the cilantro, and salt and pepper. Add a little cooking water if the salsa seems too dry.

RONSTADT FAMILY MEATBALLS | ALBONDIGAS DE LA FAMILIA RONSTADT

My grandmother made this dish most days for my grandfather when he came home from the hardware store for a hot lunch. I loved having it for dinner at my grandparents' house. My grandmother set an elegant table, and these delicate albondigas, made fragrant with mint and cilantro, were often the soup course. The *New York Times* printed this recipe in 1989 with an article about my dad.

Makes about 65 meatballs, or 6 to 8 servings.

> 3 pounds ground beef, preferably flank and round steak
>
> 6 medium-sized tomatoes, preferably plum
>
> ½ cup fresh mint, finely chopped
>
> ½ cup cilantro, minced
>
> 1 small garlic clove, minced
>
> 1 medium scallion, minced
>
> 2 tablespoons oregano
>
> Salt and pepper to taste
>
> ¾ cup olive oil or melted lard
>
> 6 cups boiling water
>
> Lime wedges for serving

Put the ground beef in a large bowl.

Broil the fresh tomatoes just until the skin can be removed easily. Peel the tomatoes and remove the seeds. Purée in a blender. There should be about 1½ cups.

Add the mint, cilantro, garlic, scallion, oregano, salt, and pepper to the meat. Mix well. Add the tomatoes and knead the mixture.

Add the oil or melted lard, incorporating it into the meat mixture by kneading. The mass should be neither dry nor too liquid. Test the mixture by forming a piece into a ball the size of a walnut. It should hold together.

Proceed to form walnut-sized balls, and then drop a few at a time into boiling water. Cook for 5 to 8 minutes. Serve the meatballs in the liquid in which they were cooked, with lime wedges on the side.

There are many variations of this traditional Sonoran soup with albondigas, or meatballs. My grandmother's simple recipe skipped the carrots, zucchini, and potatoes in the version above.

BEEF WITH CHILE | CARNE CON CHILE

This version of a classic Sonoran dish is adapted from an old Ronstadt family recipe, with one important change. Instead of store-bought chile paste in a jar, it calls for homemade red chile sauce. It's much better this way.

1 2-to-3-pound beef brisket, trimmed of excess fat and cut into 2-inch chunks

2 large yellow onions, quartered

3 or 4 bay leaves

3 or 4 garlic cloves

2 teaspoons whole peppercorns

¼ cup olive oil

¼ cup flour

4 cups red chile sauce (p. 30)

Salt and pepper to taste

Put the brisket in a large Dutch oven or heavy-bottomed soup pot with a lid and add water to cover. Add the onions, the bay leaves, all but one of the garlic cloves, and the peppercorns. Bring to a boil, then lower the heat and simmer, covered, until the meat is fall-apart tender, about 4 to 6 hours.

Remove the meat to a large bowl or platter to cool, saving the cooking broth. Cut or shred the meat into bite-sized chunks.

Put the oil in a large frying pan over medium heat. Add the last garlic clove, crushed or put through a garlic press, and sauté for a minute or so. Add the flour and cook, stirring constantly, until golden. Add the red chile sauce and cook, stirring, for about 5 minutes. Add a little of the cooking broth and stir until the sauce is thick and smooth, like gravy.

Pour the sauce over the chunks of meat and toss to coat. Don't add too much sauce. (Jackie Ronstadt's recipe warns: "Make sure carne con chile is moist—not drowned!")

The carne con chile is now ready to serve by itself, or spooned into large flour tortillas, or with beans and salsa, or with eggs for breakfast. It's best when made a day ahead.

Carne con chile with fried beans and rice.

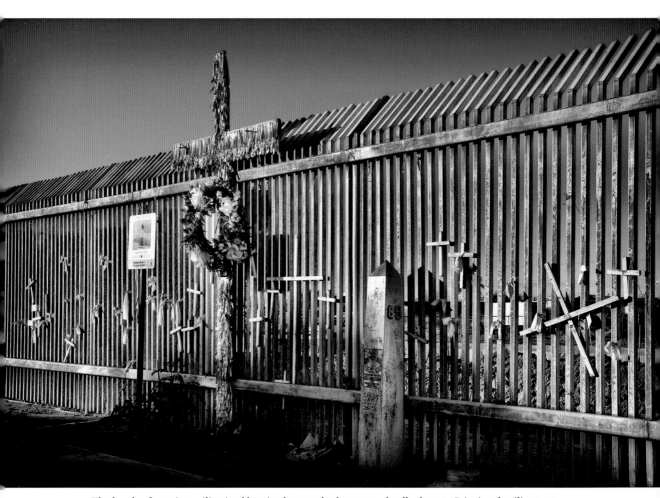

The border fence is a militarized barricade stretched across a deadly desert. Grieving families turn sections of it into a monument to love and sacrifice.

5

LA FRONTERA

WHEN I WAS A GIRL YOU COULD GET ACROSS the line easily. The border station in Nogales was a small building with a turnstile. It took a few minutes and across you went. We'd go down from Tucson for shopping in Nogales or for road-trip vacations or for social functions like pachangas. And people came up from Sonora to shop and do business on our side. We all crossed the line.

Mexican ranchers and farmers were a big part of my dad's business. They came up to Ronstadt Hardware for pumps, windmills, and other heavy equipment, and for tools and rifles and kitchenware and whatever other supplies they needed. And my dad would go to them. He drove all over Sonora to meet his Mexican customers, and sometimes he'd take me along.

I learned about the desert driving back and forth with Daddy pointing stuff out. He knew that area like the back of his hand. We'd be in the middle of the desert, driving for hours with nothing in sight, and he'd say, "Well, around this next little corner, you're going to see Don So-and-so. He's going to ask me if I want a little whiskey, and I'm going to stop and have a little drink with him."

And there the man would be, sitting on his chair by the road. He'd see my dad and say, "Un whisquito?" and my dad would go, "Sure, why not?" I'd stay in the car and they would talk business for a while. Maybe he needed a new cultivator or a windmill or something like that. My dad knew all the ranchers. They knew what he could supply, what kind of price he would give them, and that he was going to treat them fairly.

Sometimes we'd all go to Sonora as a family, singing harmonies in the car. That was before there was air-conditioning in cars. Our vacation trips were super hot and dusty, but with great food. We would stop in Hermosillo and little towns like Caborca and Oquitoa and end up in Guaymas, a fishing town on the Sea of Cortés. We would marvel at the ocean. I had never seen so much water. My father would hire a boat, we'd all go fishing, get la turista—Montezuma's revenge—throw up, and go home all sunburned. It was wonderful.

We went down for special occasions, too. Hermosillo would have a black-and-white ball for the debutantes of ranchers' families, and many Tucson families would be invited as well. The connections between Tucson and Sonora went deep because, until relatively recently, Tucson *was* Sonora. With the Treaty of Guadalupe Hidalgo, in 1848, the United States took possession of more than half of Mexico's territory, including California, New Mexico, Texas, Colorado, Nevada, Utah, and a big chunk of Arizona. In 1853, the Gadsden Purchase moved the border again, fixing the line below Tucson. Even then, the line remained fuzzy, and more work was needed to pin down exactly where Mexico ended and the United States began. It's little wonder that southern Arizona kept close affinity with Sonora, and that all kinds of connections—economic, cultural, and familial—continued to bind both places together.

When I went back to Sonora from Tucson in the 1990s, I saw what the border fence had become. It wasn't a chain-link afterthought anymore. Now it was an ugly scar, a gash in the landscape that made you feel like you were doing something bad when you crossed in either direction, there was so much fear and tension.

The border in Ambos Nogales—what they call the two Nogaleses, American and Mexican—used to be a formality between neighbors who got along. It was rich on one side and poor on the other, but the rich side wasn't always so frightened. It saw no need to fortify itself against its poorer, weaker companion.

But that was long ago. The fence has gotten hulking and monumental. Under the forty-fifth president the wall was extended in both directions and draped, in Nogales and other places, with parallel coils of lethal concertina wire. A little desert border town suddenly looked like a cross between 1950s Berlin and a supermax federal prison.

The construction was a disaster for the Sonoran Desert. Wall-building crews scraped and bulldozed miles of pristine desert floor into bare dirt track on either side of the barrier. They drained springs and aquifers, stealing life-giving water from plants and animals, to mix concrete. Quitobaquito Springs, a sacred spot for Native peoples and a rich oasis for wildlife, was depleted. Enormous saguaros, which take decades to mature, were toppled and piled and left to rot. What the crews left behind—a thirty-foot wall—stops many migrating and grazing animals in their tracks, endangering their survival.

Because of the wall and the Border Patrol, with its trucks and drones and floodlights and sensors, many migrants end up stalled in Mexican Nogales. Migrants caught on the American side are dumped there without money or prospects. People seeking refuge, who were ordered by the United States to remain in Mexico while they wait for their asylum hearings, bide their time in grimy tent camps. Migrants

The fortified border is a scar and an abomination.

who are determined to keep going wait in Nogales until they are ready to cross—to try their luck for the first time, the second, or the tenth. All the while, they are vulnerable to robbery and kidnapping by the narco gangs and human traffickers who control the northbound routes, and to the abuses of the Border Patrol waiting on the other side.

And yet, in the heart of Mexican Nogales, in the middle of all this ugliness, there is an outpost of love and human decency. It's known as the Comedor, Spanish for the dining room. It's run by the Kino Border Initiative, a partnership of Catholic sisters and priests and laypeople from both sides of the border. Migrants are welcomed there.

They arrive weary and stunned by exposure to the elements and raw from their encounters with immigration authorities, known as la migra. Their feet are blistered and bleeding; they have other injuries and traumas. Many of the women and girls have been sexually assaulted. And that is just the damage from the journey of the last few days and weeks, piled atop the terrors of the lives they fled.

The migrants get the basics. Volunteers keep the Comedor supplied with donated clothing and diapers, toothbrushes, soap, and, most important, clean, dry socks. But maybe the most restorative thing the migrants receive is a hot meal. Eggs and tortillas and beans and salsa for breakfast. For lunch, chicken in mole or menudo, the rich stew made of tripe and hominy, a fragrant, steamy bowl garnished with lime and cilantro.

The Comedor began humbly, as an improvised effort by several Catholic nuns who fed deported migrants outdoors, near a bridge by the Mariposa port of entry. The sisters then worked alongside the Jesuits to establish an indoor shelter that could give migrants food and other necessities and services. The Comedor has been doing its vital work since 2008.

I first visited there with my friend Shura Wallin, one of a group of volunteers from suburban Tucson who have supported the Comedor for many years, collecting donations of food and clothing, greeting migrants, helping them to adjust to the place, learning their stories, answering their questions, and easing their fear through simple kindness. I met Shura through my brother Mike, who had gone with Shura's

Razor wire along the border fence makes a Nogales neighborhood feel like a prison yard.

group on one of their regular searches of the Arizona side of the desert to find and help migrants who were lost or abandoned and in danger of dying.

Shura, who is in her eighties, is tiny, almost elfin, with close-cropped gray hair, boundless energy, and an uncanny ability to spot people in trouble. She speaks little Spanish beyond the basics like "amigos," a word she would call out over and over when she walked the dusty trails beside the highway, looking for migrants who might be injured or sick.

Shura solves problems. She will meet somebody in the Comedor and learn he has a toothache, then find a guy with a car who can drive him to the dentist, and then work her magic to persuade the dentist to do the work at no charge. She'll coax a friend to help fill a migrant's blood-pressure prescription at a Walgreens on the American side. She'll let migrants use her phone to call their families so they know their loved ones are alive.

Many of the migrants who visit the Comedor are determined to keep pressing on, beyond Nogales, past the wall, to jobs and families in the United States. They are aiming at Tucson, seventy-two miles up Interstate 19. The drive takes about an hour. The walk takes about a week. It's dangerous, and not just because of the Border Patrol. No one knows how many thousands of migrants have died in the Arizona desert; many bodies are unidentified, and many are never found. Volunteer groups such as No More Deaths try to lower the death toll by leaving lifesaving caches of water and food in the desert. Border Patrol agents are known to empty and destroy the water jugs when they find them. Sometimes they arrest and charge humanitarian aid-givers for sheltering and transporting migrants. Advocacy groups who keep track of the reported deaths—the corpses who are turned over to medical examiners in Tucson—mark maps with red dots that cluster all along the Arizona border, and thickly in the Tohono O'odham lands, which are sparsely populated and all the more dangerous for their isolation.

Those dots sprayed out across southern Arizona look like a map of a disease outbreak, and in a sense they are. They show the results of the disease of exclusion and hostility. Each dot is a story of hope and reckless courage that ended terribly.

CASA ALITAS

Whenever I'm back in Tucson, the first person I call is Katya Peterson. She is one of my oldest Tucson friends, tall and slender with crinkly russet hair and eyes that crinkle too, especially when she is smiling, which is most of the time. She has energetic enthusiasm that she carries with her everywhere. She is exuberant and unreserved and doesn't hold back—the kind of civic-minded soul who moves swiftly from observing and reacting to actually doing. She has her mother's force of will to make good things come about.

On my visit to Tucson in 2019, Katya invited me to make a late-afternoon trip to a place we both knew from childhood, the Benedictine Sanctuary of Perpetual Adoration, on North Country Club Road and designed by Tucson's premier architect, Roy Place. It was a Roman Catholic convent from 1940 until 2018. I wanted to see what had become of it since the sisters moved out.

Katya picked me up at the Arizona Inn and, on the short drive over, filled me in.

"The last group came in twenty or thirty minutes ago," she said. "That first line of processing has happened. Then we start to ask them more questions. Imagine how many people—Spanish is not their first language. So we've got Mam, we've got Q'eqchi', we've got Popti', we've got Kaqchikel, there's K'iche'. There are twenty-two languages just in Guatemala."

The former convent was a sanctuary again, now an improvised shelter for migrants who have been released—the better word is dumped—by Immigration and Customs Enforcement. Most were women and children from Central America. Of the thousands who fled to the southern border, these were luckier than most. ICE had let them go, to join relatives or other sponsors around the country until their asylum cases were heard. At the shelter, run by Catholic Community Services with help from volunteers, they would stay a day or two, getting their bearings. Casa Alitas, which means House of Wings, was there to provide hot meals, showers, beds, backpacks full of new clothes and toiletries, and bus tickets for the journey's next leg.

The monastery loomed over its low-rise neighborhood, a Spanish Revival landmark in pink stucco, with clay-tile roofs and a turquoise tiled dome. Beside it was a garden with orange, date, olive, and avocado trees. Above one intricately carved door, the word "Pax." A wooden "Welcome" sign hung outside, though the sisters who had put it there were gone.

The Benedictine Sisters of Perpetual Adoration had lived in the monastery for almost eighty years. They were more or less cloistered, serving meals to the homeless and staying afloat by selling tea, soaps, liturgical vestments, and gourmet popcorn. Like other congregations, they grew old and dwindled. Only a few years before, the final sixteen or so sisters had sold the place to a local developer, sold or given away furniture and paintings, then retreated to their order's home base in Missouri. The developer was planning to build apartments, but while the monastery sat empty he offered it to the shelter organizers, rent-free, to house the migrants.

Migrant men chatted and smoked beside some orange trees as Katya and I pulled up. Little boys on bicycles with training wheels clattered by. We sat in the pews of the barren chapel—no altar, no statues—while the shelter's lead coordinator, Diego Javier Piña Lopez, told its story.

ICE, he said, had long been dumping migrants without warning across the state: in desolate Yuma, at the Tucson bus station, at

McDonald's. Each time, Catholic Community Services and local families scrambled. They found houses and motel rooms and volunteers to bring food and do laundry.

As the migrants kept coming, the need for shelter kept outgrowing available space. About three weeks before our visit, to everyone's great relief, Diego got the keys to the monastery.

As he led us on a tour, that day's newly arrived migrants oriented themselves, too. A woman and a little girl came by, looking for diapers. A man in a towel dashed from the shower room to the sleeping quarters.

On the walls were maps and national flags, bus charts marked with destinations and departure times, and children's drawings: a donkey, rabbits, flowers, a resurrected Christ. Kitchen volunteers washed dishes and stirred giant pots of beans. In one room were stacks of Red Cross blankets. In another, large butcher-paper drawings covered the wall of a

Families leave mementos at the border for migrants who died trying to cross.

makeshift infirmary. They were crude outlines of human forms, with body parts marked in English and various Indigenous languages, so migrants could show a nurse or doctor where it hurt. ("Jolom" is "head" in Q'eqchi'.) Somebody had found garment racks at a defunct Kmart, so now no one had to root through trash bags for donated clothes. I talked for a while with a pediatrician. Diego proudly told us how, room by room, he and the staff and volunteers had been imposing order on chaos. Here the migrants could have at least a day or two of respite and calm after arriving traumatized and bewildered.

To cross the border is to risk a horrible death, but thousands who take that risk see no better choice. Each cross represents a migrant who died. The graffiti on the fence in Nogales reads: "Las paredes vueltas de lado son puentes." ("Walls turned on their side are bridges.")

The bewilderment was usually ICE's fault. "Even to this day, we'll have families being dropped off here and they [ICE] won't explain who we are or anything," Diego said. "So they still think we're part of immigration, we're part of ICE, and not trust us initially. So we have to work toward getting people's trust and understanding."

"There's a process," Katya told me. "We give them some different papers that they'll need, do a short interview, they go see a doctor or a nurse or somebody, to see—are you pregnant, do you have lice, do you have scabies, do you have something serious? Tuberculosis? This little girl yesterday, her whole jaw started to go like that" —she mimed a swollen cheek—"she's got a huge infection."

"Then usually they get something to eat, because at ICE they've had rarely anything for the last two days—"

"Green bologna sandwiches on Wonder Bread," I said.

"If even that. It's very haphazard how they treat them. Sometimes they give them crackers."

I have many old memories of the convent as it used to be, starting when I was a girl. It was a place of wonder, so beautiful and so pink, in the style of Egyptian Art Deco. It had a long cathedral echo, which was magical for me. We were from a different parish, Saints Peter & Paul, but that church wasn't nearly as nice. So sometimes my dad would take us there for a Christmas service or to visit the nativity scene. It was a chance to see something mystical and splendid.

I visited the convent again in the 1990s, when I had a home in Tucson and my children, Mary and Carlos, were little. I had heard that the nuns were singing chant at Vespers, so I asked their superior, Sister Dawn, if I could sing with them. I thought it was going to be Gregorian chant, but Sister Dawn explained that they didn't sing in Latin anymore, just in English. It was beautiful anyway. I used to visit a couple of times a week, just to be quiet and ease my mind. It was very peaceful, and I'd feel serene when I got home and had to deal with my kids again.

The visit with Katya haunted me. I was struck by how vulnerable the migrants were, how defenseless. How they were anything but a threat. I remember meeting a tiny woman who came up to my nose, carrying a big child, and I thought, She must have carried him all the way from Guatemala. And the sheer bewilderment of having to deal with all these languages not your own and people trying to communicate while not being able to speak Spanish or English, just being stranded, nowhere, far from family and any kind of support system. Seeing that can break your heart.

But I was glad to see the convent become a sanctuary again. This was typical of Tucson—the more progressive part of Arizona, where people I've known all my life have stepped up to meet the humanitarian emergency. I wring my hands and complain: "Oh, no, they're doing this horrible thing at the border, they're taking children away from their parents, what can we do?" But Katya's on it, and Tucson has a lot of people like her. Her family, too. Katya's daughter Anna, a doctor, is the medical director at Casa Alitas. She helps people there at all hours, on top of her full-time job.

Not long after my visit, the shelter had to move out. The developer went in and tore down buildings and dug up the orchard, and now there are ugly apartments on either side of the historic church. The deconsecration of Tucson architecture plows ahead. But so does Casa Alitas, which now works out of a former juvenile detention center, helping all the migrants it can, for as long as they keep coming.

RECIPES

✳ ✳ ✳

POT BEANS | FRIJOLES DE LA OLLA

Behold, the workhorse recipe of every Mexican household, in Sonora and beyond. This recipe is for cooking on a stovetop; using a Mexican-style clay bean pot is ideal, if you're lucky enough to have one. Just make sure to keep an eye on the water level so the beans don't scorch. Slow cookers and pressure cookers also work very well. Presoaking the beans isn't necessary. And don't salt them at first—wait until they are tender, usually after about 2 hours of simmering. Otherwise the beans will be tough.

1 pound rinsed dried beans (pintos are a Sonoran staple, but feel free to use red, black, Mayocoba, kidney, great northern, or other beans)

1 white onion, roughly chopped

2 tablespoons lard, vegetable oil, or bacon or chorizo drippings

1½ tablespoons salt, or to taste

Into a large Dutch oven or heavy-bottomed soup pot or clay bean pot put the beans and enough water to cover them by 3 inches. Add the onion and lard, oil, or drippings and bring to a boil. (If using vegetable oil, the chef Rick Bayless suggests frying the onions in the oil first, for about 10 minutes, for better flavor.) Lower the heat and simmer until the beans are completely soft. This could be a couple of hours, or more if the beans are old. Always keep the water about an inch above the beans.

When the beans are tender, add salt and cook for about 15 minutes more.

FRIED BEANS | FRIJOLES REFRITOS

Being fried, preferably in pork fat, is one of the many paths to perfection that beans travel in Mexico. But don't call these beans "refried." That is a bad translation of "refrito," which means "well fried," not "fried again."

> 2 tablespoons lard, vegetable oil, or bacon or chorizo drippings
>
> 1 medium white onion, chopped
>
> 4 garlic cloves, minced
>
> 4 cups cooked and drained beans, with cooking liquid reserved (p. 139)
>
> Salt to taste

In a large frying pan, cast-iron or nonstick, heat the lard, oil, or drippings over medium heat, then add the onion and cook, stirring, until golden, about 10 minutes. Stir in the garlic and cook for about 1 minute. Using a slotted spoon, add about 1 cup of the beans and mash them into a coarse paste with a potato masher or the back of a spoon. Keep adding and mashing the rest of the beans, 1 cup at a time, until you're done. Stir in enough cooking liquid, about ¼ cup at a time, to make the beans smooth and not chunky. (Aim for a mashed-potato consistency, says chef Rick Bayless.) The beans may be slightly soupy at this point, but they will thicken as they sit. (Don't we all.) Taste for salt and serve.

If you want to make these beans even more delicious, do as the Sonorans do and add cheese. Lucy's El Adobe Cafe in Los Angeles was one of my favorite Mexican restaurants in the '70s. My dear friend Patty Casado and her mother, Lucy, ran it for many years. They melted Colby and Monterey Jack cheese into their frijoles refritos, which gave the beans a great flavor. For this recipe, use about two handfuls of shredded cheese, in a ratio of about one-third Colby to two-thirds Monterey Jack. Once the beans are mashed, add the cheese a handful at a time, stirring until completely melted. Or you could simply put the cheese on top of a bowl or plate of beans and melt it under the broiler for a minute.

Beans, tortillas, tacos, roasted chiles, guacamole, chiltepín salsa—all the parts of a Sonoran family feast.

I don't have a place in Tucson anymore; I sold my home there a few years ago and became a full-time Californian again. My hometown remains in my thoughts and heart, though; the nostalgic shadow the place casts on me grows only longer from being farther away. Luckily for me, I keep close connections with my beloved borderlands through my far-flung family and my friendships with people there whose lives and work I deeply admire, and who aren't going anywhere. These include the volunteer heroes who help migrants along the border; they are examples of humanity at its kindest. I'm amazed at how brave and upbeat they remain in the face of shocking cruelty. Then there are gardeners and farmers, the ones who sow and weed and reap, the optimists on a smoldering planet, who are keeping hope alive, one fig grove, wheat field, and stand of agaves at a time. The ranchers, too, raising sturdy animals for meat and wool as their ancient forebears did. And the artisans in clay and wood. And, of course, the musicians.

These friends and family members love this region and I love them; I love how they embrace their community and make it better, conjuring—as our desert ancestors did—beauty from harshness. They are what keeps my Sonoran song from being an act of stale memory. They keep me grounded and connected there, and I cherish what I learn from them, all the things that are new and strange and lovely and blooming every season, day in and day out.

I've included some of them in these next few chapters.

The Mission Garden, on the west side of Tucson, takes the long, long view of the city's history.

6

THE MISSION GARDEN

THE MIGRANTS AND REFUGEES who pass through my hometown don't usually stay for long. But I'm glad that a few are able to find shelter and solace in the short time they are there, thanks to some good people in Tucson who deploy compassion and understanding to help their fellow creatures survive in a hostile place. A desert needs its oases. There's another place on the edge of town that does much the same thing: summoning beauty from ugliness.

Sentinel Peak is a cone of volcanic rock and ash that looms over the west side of Tucson. It's also called "A" Mountain, for the giant painted stone letter that University of Arizona football fans built on its upper slope more than a hundred years ago. The "A" is tacky, but it's considered historic, so we're stuck with it. Even with the blemish, the mountain is impressive—pleasingly symmetrical and bristling with saguaros. And when you're at the top it's like desert CinemaScope: the whole city lies at your feet. It's no wonder people love to hike and drive up and linger at the summit.

I like the bottom even better. There, between the foot of "A" Mountain and the Santa Cruz River, lies one of Tucson's greatest treasures: the Mission Garden, a plot of land so lusciously planted with heritage fruit trees and shrubs, cactuses and vines, vegetables and grains, all you want to do is plop under one of its shady arbors, eat some figs, and stay forever, along with the chickens and butterflies and any roadrunners who drop by.

The area is called Tucson's birthplace, and for good reason. People have been living and growing food in that very spot on the Santa Cruz's floodplain for at least four thousand years. The first evidence of farming there dates to about 2100 BC.

The Hohokam people lived there in the Middle Ages, building canals off the river to water their corn, squash, and beans. Later came the Pima and Tohono O'odham people. The O'odham called their community S-cuk Son, pronounced "chuk-shon," which has been translated as "spring at the base of the black mountain." When the Jesuit priest Eusebio Kino arrived, he wrote it down as "Tucson." The Spaniards built a mission in the area, San Agustín, with a garden and granary and other buildings. The mission eventually went to ruin and was abandoned, though Mexican farmers continued to till and plant beside the river, and Chinese immigrants and their descendants grew fruits and vegetables on the site into the 1930s. The soil was always good.

In the 1950s, the place was a dump, literally. Tucson city fathers, with a historical blindness typical for the time, bulldozed the ruins and started piling trash there. In the '70s they considered a highway that would have buried the site again, probably forever, under blacktop, but historians, archeologists, newspaper writers, and other concerned citizens spoke up. For years Tucsonans have kept destruction at bay while the city has kicked around redevelopment ideas—a heritage park and greenway beside the Santa Cruz, a rebuilt mission and Indian village, a cultural center.

Those dreams have never been fully realized. But one that did come true was the Mission Garden, restored within the footprint of the old Spanish garden as an agricultural museum, a living tribute to S-cuk Son and San Agustín. Within its adobe walls, Tucson locals and out-of-town visitors, schoolchildren and homegrown exiles like me get to see, smell, and taste a little of the Sonoran world as Native peoples and the Spaniards knew it.

The Mission Garden is green and good and helps the community, so, naturally, Katya Peterson is involved. She is an old hand at urban gardens; before moving back home, she helped create and run a well-loved community garden on the West Side of Manhattan. She is a co-director of Friends of Tucson's Birthplace, the nonprofit that supports the Mission Garden. The hard work of breathing life into the dust of a neglected garbage pile has been a community effort for years, and the garden's staff

TOP: Cholla cactuses in bloom at the Mission Garden. **BOTTOM:** Heirloom barley in the garden.

and volunteers are some of the most creative, openhearted, green-thumbed people in southern Arizona.

I went there not long ago with Katya and Dena Cowan, the garden's curator of collections. It was an early evening in spring and the garden was busting out. In the native-plant area, Dena showed us the extravagant array of cactuses, such as the prickly pears, their thorny paddles topped with delicate blossoms of sunflower yellow, soon to become fruit. The flowers on a thorn-spiked buckhorn cholla were amazingly delicate: silky pale yellow and green with filaments of red and pink. The sticklike ocotillos had blossomed already, and the agaves were hunkered down, solid and low to the ground, surrounding a roasting pit.

Dena Cowan (left), the Mission Garden's curator of collections, with Emily Rockey, the garden supervisor.

The Mission Garden is a working garden; the plants aren't there just to look pretty. Agave was an important food for the Hohokam people, and the hearts, when roasted, are starchy and nutritious, like sweet potatoes. The garden has solar ovens to bake bread and a hand-operated stone mill for grinding mesquite flour. Many people think the sturdy, stumpy mesquite tree is mainly good for charcoal and fence posts, but it's a food plant, too. Horses and cattle love to eat mesquite pods right from the tree. Dried and ground into flour, the pods become a sweetly scented superfood.

The Mission Garden might be the best place in Tucson to learn how generous the desert can be to those who respect it and know how to live within it. It's like a four-acre library of human ingenuity and tenacity, showing how people over thousands of years have learned to extract all they need from a hot, harsh world—food, medicine, clothing, shelter, and other basics, but also beauty, comfort, intoxication, and delicious flavor.

The Hohokam section of the garden grows ancient crops like squash, cotton, tepary beans, and tobacco. In the O'odham area you'll find amaranth, a wildly nutritious desert green the O'odham call "rain spinach," and the Chinese garden grows bitter melon and loofah vines and jujube trees. The Mexicans are represented by chiles and corn, and the Spanish by grapevines, an orchard of citrus, olive, quince, and fig trees, and small fields of barley and wheat. Katya pointed out a fig tree my family donated in memory of my father. Dena showed me a prickly pear from Las Delicias, the ranch in Sonora where my grandfather was born. She picked some favas, their giant fuzzy pods like funky overgrown peas, and some sweet loquats for us to eat, peel and all.

Diagonally through the garden runs an acequia, a replica of the irrigation channels the Sonorans have dug since ancient times to send river water to their crops. This one is home to some Gila topminnows, desert natives that became endangered when the rivers got polluted and dried up. They are plain-looking little fish, modest but metaphorically appropriate: like most everything else in the garden, they are sturdy survivors, stubbornly resilient and greatly underestimated.

Looking out at Tucson from "A" Mountain, with the Mission Garden in the foreground.

Some unsatisfied visitor once gave the Mission Garden a cranky one-star review on Instagram: "It's just plants." Well, yeah. Plants. Blooming in the desert. On a reclaimed dump, in a place that has sustained human lives and livelihoods for thousands of years. Meanwhile, the City of Tucson managed to keep its football "A" painted and neatly maintained for a hundred years, most of that time failing to see the priceless treasure right next to it, buried under trash. Thank goodness for the Tucsonans who stepped up and said yes to plants. If the Garden of Eden had an address, it would be 946 West Mission Lane, Tucson, Arizona, 85745.

RECIPES

✽ ✽ ✽

TEPARY BEANS | FRIJOLES TÉPARIS

The tepary bean isn't much known outside the borderlands. It's a desert plant, cultivated in Arizona and Sonora since antiquity, that thrives in conditions that would wither other crops. The hotter and drier the better, which makes this gnarly little bean, with its extra-long taproot, perfect for inclusion in this book.

As you might expect of such an arid soul, the tepary benefits from a long soak before cooking: 12 hours or overnight. It has a memorable nutty taste, holds up well in salads, and mashes like velvet for dips and soups. I know I'm singing to the choir in the Southwest, where people have championed teparies for decades, but this is a really good bean.

It has long seemed to be on the brink of becoming famous and popular, but it never quite gets there. In 1912, at the International Dry-Farming Congress in Alberta, Canada, the tepary was honored for the obvious reasons, but even that, plus an endorsement from the well-known baked-bean company Van Camp's, wasn't enough.

Why? People have theories. The Arizona ethnobotanist Gary Paul Nabhan, a giant in the field of beans, wrote his master's thesis on teparies, and he says part of what may be holding them back is their reputation for unwanted side-effects.

Lawrence asked him to explain, and Gary sent back a helpful email:

> Most people undercook them, since they take longer than most dry beans, and folks don't realize that. . . . After writing parts of two books and a dozen papers on beans, it's clear that teparies have lots of soluble and insoluble fiber compared with lentils and favas, and that creates too much gas for the faint of heart. That may be why desert ranchería villages in the Río Sonora have houses scattered farther apart than in the New Mexican pueblos . . . to let the bean gas fly where it may. That's a sort of culinary determinism of settlement patterns, but is only idle conjecture.

Maybe it will take our new world of endless drought for this underappreciated bean to finally join the mainstream. But don't hold your breath. (Or maybe do hold your breath.) If you want to try teparies in the meantime, you can buy them online at nativeseeds.org. Use 8 cups of water to 1 cup of beans, and boil them patiently until they are completely tender, which could take up to 4 hours. Then use them as you would in any recipe for pinto or other beans.

SAUTÉED WILD GREENS | QUELITES SALTEADOS

Quelites is a catchall word in Sonora for varieties of wild greens, like amaranth, lambsquarters, and purslane. You can call them by their other name, weeds, but that would be insulting and ill-informed. Desert people, at least, can appreciate these nutrient-dense, delicious plants that show up without being asked, free for the picking. Finding them—and they can be easy to find, if you know where and when to look—is like catching nature in an unexpectedly indulgent mood. The only downside is that quelites seasons can be frustratingly short.

In his essential book *Gathering the Desert*, a catalog of Sonora's edible abundance, the ethnobotanist Gary Paul Nabhan tells how amaranth and other wild greens once sustained the Tohono O'odham in the central Sonoran Desert. They planted in the floodplains when the summer rains arrived, but then they had to wait a couple of months. Meanwhile, they had quelites. Amaranth is sometimes called pigweed, but the Tohono O'odham have a much better name: "rain spinach."

"Before the crops matured," Nabhan writes, "volunteering amaranths, lambsquarters, purslane, and annual saltbush greens were the major products harvested from Papago [Tohono O'odham] fields. Some families would fix amaranths frequently when they were around, as salad, or as boiled or fried greens, as a filling with beans in fat little corn tortillas, or in a mixture with meat or eggs."

Quelites are often sautéed and added to something else, like meat or beans. Look for lambsquarters, amaranth, and purslane in a Mexican market or your backyard. Spinach and other spinachy greens like chard, collards, and dandelion greens will also work in this recipe. You can blanch quelites first in boiling water if you like; they will cook up softer and quicker.

8 cups quelites, well-washed and dry

3 tablespoons vegetable oil or lard

4 garlic cloves, thinly sliced

3 green Anaheim or poblano chiles

3 tablespoons flour

4 spring onions

1 cup cooked and drained beans, like pinto or red beans

Salt to taste

Wash the quelites well, chop them into 1-inch pieces, and set them aside. In a large saucepan, heat the oil or lard on medium heat and add the garlic. Sauté until soft and golden and remove to a small bowl. Add the peppers to the pan and brown them, being careful not to burn them. (If you do they will taste bitter.) Remove them to the bowl with the garlic.

Add flour to the saucepan, and cook, stirring constantly, until lightly browned. Add the spring onions and cook until translucent. Add the quelites, letting them shrivel a little before adding the cooked garlic and peppers and the beans. Lower the heat to medium-low. Taste and add salt if necessary. Cook until the greens are just tender. Serve with hot flour or corn tortillas.

Quelites made with bledos and nopalitos—wild amaranth greens and prickly-pear cactus paddles.

The main buildings of the Canelo Project, with Turkey Creek in the foreground.

7
CANELO DIARY

THE CANELO PROJECT, the home and compound of my friends Athena and Bill Steen, is not a civic project like the Mission Garden or Casa Alitas. It's pretty far from Tucson, and it wasn't something I knew about growing up, but it's one of those strange and special places I treasure and visit as often as I can. I want to share it because of what it has shown me about living well with beauty and simplicity. I imagine my great-grandparents would have been baffled by some of it, but I think they would have understood it overall.

Canelo seems to have emerged from deep in the earth, either from being thrust upward by geologic forces or slowly exposed through long erosion.

It also looks like it could have been built by some vanished band of pre-Columbian artisans with strikingly modern taste, and who knew a little about Japan and psychedelia along with timber framing and thatching. Or maybe the local bears and javelinas built it, somehow creating from all this dirt and stone a place beautifully fit for human habitation and contemplation.

When you take it all in, it's good to go slowly, meandering the grounds, as I've done many times over many years.

Gaze at the adobe and straw-bale dwellings and walls and walkways and various sinuous structures that could be functional or purely sculptural but are probably both. Stroll among the shimmying cottonwoods and emory oaks and prickly-pear cactuses and quince trees, noting everywhere the artful arrangements of stone, concrete, clay, and wood, and the general absence of right angles and sharp edges, except for some terracing here and clotheslines there and the parallel rows of vegetables in the garden plot. Consider how the free-form curves of packed straw and smeared earth

A sculptured window with lime plaster.

recapitulate the grassy hillsides that rolled and swelled beneath you as you drove to this place, an hour and a half southeast of Tucson and not many minutes from the Mexico border, crossing wide-open ranch land and climbing to four thousand mountainous feet and passing a ranger station of the Coronado National Forest.

You'll end up thinking, as I always do: What an earthy miracle this place is.

Of course there's nothing supernatural about the Canelo Project. It is a place for people to learn how to live on the land in sustainable grace, reconnected to one another and to the earth and the creatures around them. This they learn through workshops, where Athena and Bill and their sons teach people to build and make beautiful homes and other structures using straw, clay, and wood. After a day's work the family and guests all share stories and bottles of mescal bacanora. Canelo is, among these other things, a lovely bed-and-breakfast.

Canelo was built by two very driven, creative people who are different but quite compatible, undaunted owners of a let's-try-this-and-if-not-try-that approach to living. (Well, those two plus their kids and a community of artisanal builders and collaborators and friends that they have nurtured for many years.) Athena is an artist in clay, the daughter of an architect-potter and sister of a sculptor, all of the Santa Clara Pueblo of New Mexico. Bill has deep ties to Tucson and Sonora—Mexican and Anglo like mine—and from our great-grandparents to our children, members of our families have known one another across many generations. Bill and I are laced together at the roots.

But I didn't know that until the 1980s, when I went on a ride with my brother Mike, who was going to look at a windmill that needed fixing down near Elgin, in Santa Cruz County. Mike was then running what was left of the family hardware business, and he had a knack for meeting and befriending good people. He told me he really liked this couple in Canelo. As we pulled up in front of the house and I saw how the plantings were terraced and the way the buildings and grounds fit together, I knew instantly I'd be friends with them. I knew I was in the right place.

Later I realized that Bill's mother, Rose, was a friend of my mother's; they were in the Women's Auxiliary together. Our fathers were friends, too—Bill told me that when he and his dad went to father-son events at the Tucson Rotary Club, he often sat across from my dad.

But it goes deeper than that. Bill's grandfather was born in Banámichi. Bill thinks our great-grandfathers probably knew each other when they lived in Sonora in the mid-1800s. Their connection was Manuel María Gándara, a landowning patriarch and the governor of Sonora. For a time, my great-grandfather Friedrich Ronstadt managed Gándara's hacienda in Tepahui, keeping the books on his crops, livestock, and silver mine. Bill's great-grandfather Jean Pierre Chambon was a Frenchman living in Sonora who fought with his countrymen when France briefly conquered Mexico in the 1860s. My great-grandfather fought on the Mexican side, as colonel to General Ignacio Pesqueira.

It was good for my earthly existence that the French were driven out, because if Pesqueira had been defeated, my great-grandfather might not have survived. Bill says his great-grandfather was later killed by Apaches.

But old brutalities are forgotten when you are in Canelo; it's a place whose restful beauty can give you the sense that these borderlands are more serene than they actually are. It's an illusion, of course. The land has been fought over for centuries, and the fight over who belongs and who doesn't continues today. Driving near the Steens' property, which is close enough to Sonora for you to pick up an automated "Welcome to Mexico" text on your cellphone, you'll see Border Patrol caravans and hovering drones. Our toxic immigration politics can't be escaped, not even here. But you'll also see javelinas, neat lines of little porker babies dashing across the road behind mama. And pronghorn antelopes, wild turkeys, vultures, white-tail deer, horses, and coyotes.

The Canelo Project can give the sense of its being improvised, especially in the way its dwellings and structures, and the sense of inside and out, flow and change in and around the property. But it is also so clearly the product of years of hard work. I love its mortared stone walls, poured-in-place concrete patios with concrete-riverstone grout, and light-drenched interior spaces with banquettes and interior walls made of straw bales. The surfaces are simultaneously smooth and cool, sturdy and warm, giving an overall feel of Southwest desert permanence. Permanence—at least until the clay and adobe structures, and the people who built them, return to the soil.

Canelo is not just the buildings, where workshop participants go to learn straw-bale building and plastering and other techniques that combine structural practicality with deep attention to beauty. The Steens have a lot sunk into their project, and it's very well equipped, with workshops full of industrial power tools and various compact dwellings on the grounds equipped with all the conveniences. The compound has many comfortable places to lounge and think and read and talk and drink.

Bill refuses to take sole credit for what it's become. "The Canelo Project is a big 'We' in every respect," he said. "Neither of us, nor our kids, can be singled out when it comes to the materials, the colors, the frescos and building techniques. I

A shed for paint and plastering tools.

TOP: Bill and Athena Steen with their boys (from left), Panther, Oso, and Benito, and their dog, Ellie.
BOTTOM LEFT: A Canelo Project guest cottage.
BOTTOM RIGHT: Athena and her students made this clay plaster carving at a workshop in Slovakia.

primarily evolved the straw-bale system we use today; Athena is the plaster carver and does the beveled plaster work. But you have to add up all the pieces to get to where we are now."

Athena has a generous spirit and the soul of an artist. When you talk with her you know she's always listening. Her laugh is big and her eyes are forever smiling. She and Bill raised their kids in an unusual way, without formal schooling of any kind, but with an abundance of the other kind of education: hands-on, practical, and intuitive. Their sons—Benito; Arjuna, nicknamed Oso; and Kalin, who goes by Panther—simply went everywhere with their mom and dad, doing everything they did, building beauty out of earth, water, and straw. The boys have grown up to be impressive and intrepid adults. They have traveled the world as skilled workmen and artisans, great at improvising, and undaunted by anything.

I remember one visit to Canelo about ten years ago. Lying on my back on a bench on a cool November night. People around me drinking bacanora and murmuring in conversation while I was staring at the sky, thick with stars like spattered paint. I was pretty far from home, and as usual terrified of the dark, especially outdoors in a place as wild as this. I never like to think about what could be out there, wanting to devour me. But I was also among old and new friends in a place where I felt like I belonged from the moment I'd first arrived, more than twenty years before. I found it easy to lay my walking sticks beside me on the ground, and to let my legs and arms relax, and to savor the enveloping darkness, there among the invisible hills, suspended for a while between earth and heaven.

My friend Dennis Moroney with a couple of handsome coworkers at 47 Ranch in McNeal, Arizona.

8

DESERT CATTLE

NOT TOO FAR FROM CANELO is a cattle operation run by two friends who are the soul of gentle kindness and good humor. I am glad to say that with Deb and Dennis Moroney, of 47 Ranch, I have forged a bond that transcends my feelings about red meat.

Deb and Dennis raise Criollo cattle on their ranch in McNeal, in Cochise County, not far from Tombstone. The breed is descended from livestock that lived in North Africa and the Iberian peninsula a thousand years ago. Spanish conquistadors brought them to Mexico in the early 1500s. Criollo cattle are wiry animals, smart and curious and sturdy, and beautifully adapted to living in the desert Southwest. They have long horns to protect themselves from predators, and an amazing ability to fend and forage for themselves.

The American West is ground zero for the myth of rugged individualism, the belief that, in these wide-open spaces, people live lives of magnificent self-reliance. This is largely fiction, as any honest rancher who grazes his herds on public land and enjoys taxpayer-subsidized financing and the use of government-built infrastructure will tell you. But some creatures in the Sonoran borderlands really *are* rugged individualists, in the very best sense of that word. They are Criollo cattle, raised by a few ranchers like the Moroneys, who are building the future of sustainable agriculture by tapping into the deep, deep past.

The Moroneys' ranch is about half mountains and half desert grassland, and their cattle range all over it.

"I would say that the Criollo are exceptionally well-suited for living out here," Dennis said. "When they were evolving in North Africa, at the same latitude, they

Besides Criollo cattle, 47 Ranch also raises sheep for wool.

had access to acacia trees. They were browsing on acacias about twelve thousand or fifteen thousand years ago. I wasn't around then, but you know, they seem to be very good at making use of their resources."

Because the Criollo can eat a much more varied diet than ordinary feed-lot cattle can, they tread more lightly on the land; the desert is their salad bar. They eat mesquite in spring and various grasses in the other seasons, and cactus when they find it.

The 25,000-acre ranch has many mesquite trees. The trees have very deep roots, and when they green up in early spring, the cattle eat the emerging leaves, seedpods, and flowers, reaching up to about six feet. Around the time of the summer monsoons, the mesquites' bright-green leaves become duller and are no longer palatable. But that's when the grasses and summer annuals arrive, especially after the first good rain or two, and the Criollo shift over to those.

"I've identified more than fifty different grasses on the ranch, and that's just grasses," Dennis said. "And we've got shrubs and trees and cactus and so forth. And winter feed for our cattle includes a fair amount of prickly pear. We have photos and video of cows reaching inside of a cholla cactus and sticking their tongue way out and just licking the cholla bud out of the middle and then carefully rolling that back into their mouth and then munching it. They're amazing that way."

The Moroneys select their animals for a calm disposition and the adaptability to do well on their own. "We are low-input ranchers," Dennis said. "We don't give our cattle any insecticides, wormers, hormones, or antibiotics. They are living out there as wild as the deer."

All the Moroneys provide are trace minerals with salt blocks, and sometimes— because persistent drought has made life on the range exceptionally difficult—a nutritional supplement to help mothers with calves. Nursing takes a lot out of a cow.

"I bought a supplement," Dennis said, "sort of like a hard toffee, essentially cooked tubs of molasses. It provides protein from plant-based sources and a pretty high energy level, plus vitamins and minerals. So that will help them."

TOP: Criollo cattle live lightly on the land. **BOTTOM:** Dennis and Deb Moroney were college sweethearts before they were Arizona ranchers.

The Moroneys ride their range on horses, but four wheels are useful, too, for the difficult terrain.

The drought has brought the Moroneys one challenge after another. "Last year we only got five and a half inches of rain, and this area normally gets twelve to sixteen inches," Dennis said on a spring day in 2021. "They're holding up so far. But all the dirt tanks are dry, and we've lost cows to getting stuck in the mud. They try to get the last little bit of water and wade out into the mud and get bogged down and not able to get out."

In his cowboy hat and majestic wiry beard, Dennis looks like he stepped out of a daguerreotype, except his green reflector shades give away his hipness. He speaks in thoughtful, complete paragraphs, a fitting demeanor for life among ruminants. Deb, with her hair tied back and her buoyant smile, is as lovely as she was in college, when she was taking a modern-dance course and Dennis signed up, the only man in the class, so he could meet her.

Deb is also a medical doctor, and an accomplished knitter (the Moroneys raise sheep as well as cattle), and they both play the bongos. When they've gone with me on journeys to the Río Sonora, they have often been found dancing at the edge of the stage, twirling arm in arm and eye to eye.

Criollo beef is dark red, and tastier than supermarket commodity beef. You can find it at the Food Conspiracy Co-op in Tucson and at farmers' markets in Sierra Vista and Bisbee. Look for the name 47 Ranch, and the guy with the beard.

Oswaldo Velazquez, 8, and Natalie Caldera, 10, of Los Cenzontles Cultural Arts Academy performing "El Torero," a traditional mariachi son abajeño, in Banámichi in 2019. Oswaldo is playing the bull.

9

EL FUTURO

ONE OF MY HAPPIEST HOMECOMINGS to Tucson and Sonora happened in 2019. It was a trip that magically combined great music, delicious food, and the sweet company of many people close to my heart. It started as a trip to research the book you're holding. At first this was going to be a little family cookbook, and a few of us had planned to go down to the Río Sonora looking for things to eat. But then plans shifted a bit. The film producer James Keach, who was working on a documentary about me, asked for an on-camera interview. I said okay, on the condition that he go with me to Mexico to film it.

I had already invited my old pal Jackson Browne along. We added my cousin Bobby George and my nephew Petie and his wife, Jackie, and their little daughter, Annabelle. Word got around, and two reporters, Randy Lewis of the *Los Angeles Times* and Ernesto (Neto) Portillo of the *Arizona Daily Star*, wanted to join us. We added in spouses and partners and friends, and that's how we came to invade Sonora in a fully loaded musical motorcoach.

Our group became complete about an hour or so after we headed south out of Tucson. We stopped at a hotel in American Nogales to pick up a last load of passengers— about a couple dozen kids in matching blue hoodies, most ages eight to sixteen, along with their backpacks and suitcases and musical instruments and costumes.

Then we crossed the razor-encrusted border fence into the other Nogales, made it past the customs checkpoint, and started rolling south into Sonora. Once we hit cruising speed, everything was sunny, bright, and loud—with music bouncing around the walls and floor and ceiling.

The kids were playing jaranas and requintos and singing an old song in a traditional Mexican call-and-response style, the way people used to spread gossip across the village or over the backyard fence. One girl kept the beat on a donkey-jawbone instrument called a quijada. The song was "El Buscapiés," an old tune from Veracruz in the son jarocho style, about firecrackers that jump around on the ground looking for your feet.

The children were members of Los Cenzontles, a cultural-arts academy in the San Francisco Bay Area. I remember leaning back in my seat toward the rear of the bus and smiling, savoring the impromptu concert: These kids were good and they knew how to play traditional music right. They really understood the nuanced rhythms of those old songs. Across the aisle from me was Jackson. Like me, he has become a deep admirer of this amazing folk group. I had introduced him to them not long before, and he was taken with the children's musicianship, discipline, and soul. He got on so well with the group's founder, Eugene Rodriguez, that he immediately co-wrote a song with him and recorded it with the organization's touring band, also called Los Cenzontles.

Jackson had a ukulele and put down a half-eaten apple to play along, getting into the rhythm and spirit and quickly finding his groove within the repeating chord patterns of the son jarocho.

I've known Los Cenzontles for more than thirty years. ("Cenzontles" means "mockingbirds" in the Indigenous Mexican language Nahuatl. A poem in that language about the mockingbird's many voices inspired the name.) Eugene and his wife, Marie-Astrid, have been my dear friends for that long. At Los Cenzontles Cultural Arts Academy, kids are introduced to their shared family heritage through music and visual art. They learn their culture and roots by studying traditional songs from across Mexico and getting the training to perform them well. Los Cenzontles stresses the rigor and responsibility that musical excellence demands. Students play, sing, and dance, often in traditional costumes featuring handmade lace and embroidery. The lovely outfits—both traditional and innovative—are designed and made by Marie-Astrid, whose own heritage is French and Vietnamese.

Properly skilled and magnificently dressed, the Cenzontles embody the spirit of music and mexicanidad. It flows out of them. This happens in concerts and at outdoor fiestas—or, because the spirit and skills are portable, at home or on the road, even on a bus. I first saw them busking for change in San Francisco in the 1990s, when they were playing and dancing in the deep traditions of the son jarocho. At the time, I was touring with my mariachi show, surrounded by superb professional Mexican dancers, and I thought: These kids are the real thing. They can hold their own with the best of them.

A performance by Los Grupos Danza Xunutzi and Masehua, in Miguel Hidalgo Plaza in Banámichi.

Belinda Ortega (left) and her sister Camila of Los Cenzontles at a performance at Sacramento State University in 2018. Belinda played the pandero and Camila the quijada, a donkey jawbone.

When I worry about the future of our country, and about Mexican America, and feel in need of hope and inspiration, I can just head across a bridge to the East Bay, to a working-class, mostly Latino neighborhood called San Pablo. That's the place the Cenzontles call home. The academy is in a reclaimed liquor store that is part of a nondescript strip mall.

When you step inside, you are transported from commercial banality into a wonderland built as a place for children to dream and to flex their creative muscles. Children have profound emotions and they need ways to express them. Eugene and Marie-Astrid have given them a sacred space, bursting with possibility. Art practically drips from Marie-Astrid's fingertips, and her wall hangings and painted designs have transformed the center into a place of beauty and practical function. It is packed with musical instruments and audio and video equipment, and there is a stage and dance space, plus dressing rooms, classrooms, and a cozy, colorfully tiled kitchen, with couches and comfy chairs all around. Kids can go there after school and do their homework along with their music and art. They can eat healthy snacks and learn to make them. Parents and caregivers and siblings drop in. The streets of the East Bay can be mean; Los Cenzontles gives these mockingbirds a safe nest of their own.

For Mexican American children with their feet in two worlds—or, if you prefer, one world severed by an artificial border—that feeling of security and ownership is vital. It gives them a foundation solid enough to stand on and, more than that, to sing and dance and stomp their feet on, like the Cenzontles' traditional tarima, a small wooden platform that functions as a percussion instrument and movable stage.

"We instill in them a sense of belonging, to our Mexican heritage and to our country, the United States," Eugene once wrote. "Most educational institutions treat minority students like invited guests, however politely. But a strong sense of belonging is what best benefits children and a democratic society."

Leave it to Eugene to make the link between folk dancing and a stronger democracy. He's good at making connections, which he sees and builds and explains better than anybody. For him, the essence of folk music is independence and resourcefulness. He understands what old songs can do and how music, tradition,

Students at Los Cenzontles learn folk art as well as music. They made these traditional altars out of paper and cardboard for Día de los Muertos, with watercolor images of their deceased grandparents and the places and things they loved.

and history fit together. He finds the pathways that connect his twenty-first-century California kids to the Mexican heritage he wants them to inhabit and claim as their own.

Some of these pathways are literal. Eugene created a corrido, a Mexican story-ballad, about Juan Bautista de Anza, the Spanish explorer who in 1775 and 1776 led a group of settlers on a 1,200-mile voyage from Sonora to the San Francisco Bay. They built a fort there: the Presidio. It's a short walk from my home.

If I had the stamina and the time, and the right horse, I could saddle up at home, drop by the Presidio, then travel the Anza trail in reverse, down the length of California, through southern Arizona and northern Mexico to Arizpe, the village by the Río Sonora where Anza was born and where he lies buried in a marble crypt. The entire way, my pony and I would never leave Mexican America. Every inch of territory along the route is land that Mexicans have lived on for longer than there has been a United States.

The day our bus entered Mexico—February 15, 2019—the forty-fifth president declared a national emergency at the border.

It was a fake crisis, meant to stoke panic and anger over Central American migrants, many of them children, who were walking to Texas seeking refuge from murderous violence in their home countries. They posed no threat to the United States, but that meant nothing to the administration.

If the migrants had come in a different era, back when America had a surplus of idealism and self-confidence, when it wasn't so snarling and afraid, the way it's been at least since 9/11, these helpless children and their mothers might have been welcomed, or at least tolerated. If their skin were whiter, if they had money or were fleeing the right ideology, let's say communism, this surely would have been a different story.

Nobody in the world is more vulnerable than a refugee. She has no rights or protections in the country she left, none in the place she wants to go. America was

A vehicle barrier along the border near Douglas, Arizona.

practically invented to solve that problem, or at least that's what we Americans used to tell ourselves. But these days, the Statue of Liberty seems to be off the job.

The border "emergency," like the fortified border wall, told a very different American story. It said to people who are from south of here: We fear you and hate you and we will do all we can to keep you out.

Mexican Americans have heard this story forever, though we are hardly alone. The ideology of white supremacy excludes all kinds of people, not just us. We know we belong here, but to many white people it is a provisional belonging, subject to their tolerance and approval.

I know my father and uncles dealt with bigotry and racism as businessmen in twentieth-century Tucson. They were insulated from the worst of it by relative whiteness and relative wealth. Still, they knew their roots. In the 1960s, when Tucson was pursuing the literal erasure of Mexican identity, my dad and uncle Edward were among the Mexican American leaders who urged the city to save some of its Hispanic past, to preserve the area around the San Agustín cathedral downtown, when the forces of urban renewal were trying to bury the barrio in modern concrete. They stood up proudly to defend it.

I'm sure they both would be heartbroken to see how the country has sunk into anti-immigrant racism and horrifying violence, like the 2019 terrorist massacre at the Walmart in El Paso, one of the most Mexican cities in America. The hatred is always there, but it boils and spatters when someone is there to heat and stir the pot. We say we are a nation of immigrants, but every immigrant group has had to fight its way to inclusion—to go from outside to inside. Many are still fighting that battle. Some have forgotten it. The Irish were the Mexicans of the nineteenth century. (Well, the Mexicans were, too.) The tragedy is that many present-day descendants of immigrants look back at their own ancestors as the righteous and holy ones, and regard the newest arrivals with suspicion and disgust. We've turned Ellis Island into a sacred space and the Río Grande into a zone of terror and revulsion. Sorry, you tired Mexicans, poor Salvadorans and Guatemalans, homeless Haitians—you're too late.

It would be more honest if we called our country the United States of Who the Fuck Are You?

What to do? We can't control how others feel about us. But we have a say in how we feel about ourselves. Rejecting being devalued is half the battle. We can work to be comfortable in our own skins, to carry ourselves knowing that we belong, that this land is our land, from California to Arizona to Texas to Chicago to Alabama to the New York Island.

And that is what music and art can do. When you tap into the strength of those who came before you, those who took their love and suffering and made it music, you become strong and resilient, too. This is what Los Cenzontles is doing for their kids in San Pablo, and why I admire them so much. And likewise for artists such as La Marisoul, of the Los Angeles band La Santa Cecilia, and Los Jornaleros del Norte, a group made up of day laborers who draw on old songs and compose new ones to tackle issues both timeless and urgent, making music of great beauty and dignity.

When I made the album *Canciones de Mi Padre*, singing Mexican songs in Spanish, it wasn't as radical a departure as some made it out to be. I simply wanted to take my singing in a direction I had long wanted to go, to finally perform the songs I'd learned as a girl. It was an artistic project, not a political one. But inevitably my identity became part of it, and while some white critics initially dismissed the album as trivial exotica, the sturdy and beautiful songs spoke for themselves. The records sold by the ton, and the "Canciones" shows, with top-flight mariachi bands and dancers, were packed with audiences who knew the songs and sang along. It was thrilling and humbling to see Mexican Americans young and old embrace the records as a source of community pride—not that they needed any reason from me to feel proud of their roots and musical heritage. I felt proud to be able to honor my father and aunt Luisa and our shared Sonoran roots.

The musicianship of my mariachi touring company was exquisite. The show was full of elaborate stagecraft, with dazzling dancing and moving railroad trains and live white doves. Sometimes I sang on horseback. The music was accessible, and non–Spanish speakers could love the songs without understanding the words. With songs about cowboys and courting and desperate heartbreak, and places like Agua Prieta, Cananea, and Guaymas, audiences were getting a Sonoran education without ever knowing it. The peak of crossover instruction was probably the time I taught Elmo on *Sesame Street* how to sing a Mexican cowboy song, "La Charreada," in English with the help of some Muppet vaqueros. It wasn't a master class at Lincoln Center, but it was a lot of fun, and it showed a lot of kids how Mexicans made music that was sophisticated, buoyant, and joyful. I didn't teach Elmo the other songs in the cantina jukebox, the kind that make you want to weep into your pillow until you die.

Eugene and I differ a little on mariachis. The mariachis' traditional charro costume is the Mexican equivalent of Spanish colonial formal attire—what a wealthy landowner would wear while riding to a ball on the hacienda. That annoys Eugene, who has no patience for nineteenth-century fixations on class and caste, or working musicians trying to impress their social betters by dressing like European dandies. Eugene understands that a musician or dancer is no less impressive or lovely in a peasant dress or rebozo or handwoven sandals. To me there's nothing sharper than a handsome mariachi in a tailored, embroidered suit gleaming with silver braid and wearing a majestic sombrero. But the Cenzontles touch me deeply, and I see Eugene's point.

What matters most is that these songs get learned and played and heard and passed on. "Using old traditions to build new traditions," as Eugene and Marie-Astrid's marvelously talented son, Emiliano, has said. There's nothing dying or dead about any of this.

I adopted my children, Mary and Carlos, as newborns. Mary holds the family record as the youngest Ronstadt ever to make her mark in the recording studio. When she was a baby, I was making a children's record. I wanted to record "We Will Rock You," the Queen stadium anthem, as a lullaby. For the rhythm track, I sampled a baby's heartbeat and added the sound of Mary and her pacifier. I have a picture of her with

Los Cenzontles Traditional Mariachi (from left): Tregar Otton, Julian Gonzalez, Lucina Rodriguez, Hugo Arroyo, and Eugene Rodriguez.

her headphones on, sucking her binky for the microphone. We will (very gently) rock you. Instead of stomp-stomp clap, it was lub-dub squeak.

Mary is now grown and living on her own. She has a beautiful singing voice and a deep understanding of the traditional rhythms of old Mexican songs. She has confident command of things that took me years to learn. She's also an artist and craft maker who has filled my house with striking images and collages and mixed-media paintings, like reimagined religious icons. Animals are a recurring motif. She painted a version of Our Lady of Guadalupe, with a cat as the Madonna and, beneath her, filling in for a cherub, her own brother, Carlos, with his horn-rimmed glasses and beard. Carlos, also grown and gone, works in information technology for a big company in the Bay Area. I see the two of them and their significant others regularly at Sunday brunch at my house in San Francisco.

Back in Tucson, every third Sunday is when as many Ronstadts as possible gather at one of our houses for food and songs. They've done it for years. Covid threw a wrench in the tradition for a while, but no global pandemic was ever going to stop Third Sunday. But you don't have to be in the family to hear us play; go to Tucson any time and you'll find some Ronstadt or several Ronstadts playing around town. It could be Bobby George and Bill, or my niece Mindy, who sings and records with Bill as Mindy Ronstadt and the One-Bill Band. (It used to be the All-Bill Band, and later the Two-Bill Band, but that is another story.) My nephews—Mike's sons Mikey and Petie, and Suzy's son Kiko Jácome—are working musicians based out of Tucson. And we'll see what happens with Petie and Jackie's daughter, Annabelle. She's into Legos at the moment, but at some point soon the family destiny may seize her. Or she'll want to be a scientist, like her mom.

Petie, keeper of my grandfather's old Martin guitar, owns another family heirloom. It's a tattoo on his forearm of a Sonoran mountain ridge, taken from a watercolor painting by my father. My dad took his images from life, so somewhere down in Sonora—near Guaymas, maybe?—is the spot where he sat for a while in the hot Sonoran air with his paints and canvas and captured the jagged desert skyline. When Petie is traveling in Sonora, he'll sometimes hold his arm up to see if the mountain on his arm matches the one on the horizon. As far as I know he hasn't found it yet.

I last went to Sonora in 2019, on that bus escapade. I moved back to Tucson as an adult and lived there ten years before relocating to San Francisco, and I've been back to Tucson many times since. Climate change has made it a few degrees too hot for me to want to have a house there again, but I've thought about it. Or maybe somewhere farther south in Arizona, in the relative coolness of the sky islands, or in Banámichi. When I'm back in Tucson it doesn't feel strange, the way it did for my aunt Luisa. It feels really familiar. I have many friends there that I've never let go of. Patsy from first grade is one. And Katya and her sisters Quinta and Eva Ann. But the

TOP: Peter and Suzy dressed up for church. **BOTTOM:** Suzy in a quiet moment. She is about fifteen years old here.

fears I had are really familiar, too—the way I was afraid of the dark, of being alone in the wilderness, which Arizona has a lot more of than San Francisco. It's scary in the desert when it's pitch-dark and wide open. But when the moon lights everything up and the stars are bright and beautiful, it's magical.

Tucson remains my point of origin and the center of my soul; everything radiates out from there. Margarita and Friedrich, Lupe and Fred, and Fred's first wife, Sara, rest in Holy Hope Cemetery, on the north side of town, along with my mom and dad. Suzy died in 2015. I have a photo with her from the year before, when she came by my Tucson house to collect a garden statue. We're in the driveway, leaning over the bed of Suzy's pickup truck, having a too-rare chat, sister to sister. I miss her. And I miss Mike, who was taken far too soon, in 2016. Peter and I are plugging away.

"A la Orilla de un Palmar" is a song about a sorrowful orphan living at the edge of a palm grove. "I spend my life alone," she sings, "and alone I come and go, like the waves of the sea." If there is a more pitiable lamentation in all the Mexican songbook, I don't know what it might be.

Nor do I know where the song came from, or who in our family learned it first, but it's been passed down through generations of Ronstadts. I know my grandfather sang it, and my aunt Luisa sang it with him. Then my dad sang it, with us kids singing along. Then it was my generation's turn. From my three uncles there were three sons who sang together: a cousin trio. It was my brother Mike, my uncle Edward's son Johnny, and my uncle Bill's son Bill, in three-part harmony. They sounded just beautiful together, and when they sang it at family gatherings, everybody would join in the chorus.

A la orilla de un palmar	*At the edge of a palm grove*
Yo vi de una joven bella	*I saw a beautiful young child*
Su boquita de coral	*Her coral mouth*
Sus ojitos, dos estrellas	*Her little eyes, two stars*
Al pasar le pregunté	*In passing I asked someone*
Que quién estaba con ella	*Who was with her*
Y me respondió llorando	*And she answered me crying*
Sola vivo en el palmar	*I live alone in the palm grove*
Soy huerfanita ¡ay!	*I am an orphan, ay!*
No tengo padre ni madre	*I have no father or mother*
Ni un amigo ¡ay!	*Nor even a friend, ay!*
Que me venga a consolar	*Who might come to comfort me*
Solita paso la vida	*All alone I go through life*
A la orilla de un palmar	*At the edge of a palm grove*
Y solita voy y vengo	*And all alone I come and go*
Como las olas del mar	*Like the waves on the sea*

We would all sing it and then everybody would cry because it was so sad.

I sang "A la Orilla" on an album with the Chieftains and Ry Cooder in 2010. It was the last song I ever recorded. During the Sonora bus trip, I sat on a couch doing my best to sing it again, with Bobby George on accordion and Petie on guitar. It was a struggle, but I couldn't let my cousin and nephew sing it without me.

The song appears again in *Linda and the Mockingbirds*, a 2020 documentary that captures a lot of what I've been telling you about the Cenzontles, and about my relationship with Mexico. It's a moment that touched my heart.

Ana Cristina López Méndez, a Xunutzi dancer, wowed Jackson Browne and me in Banámichi in 2019.

When our bus traveled down the Río Sonora, we stopped for public performances by Los Cenzontles in Banámichi and Arizpe. They shared their repertoire and performed with a young folkloric dance troupe from the area.

At one performance, one of the Cenzontles teenagers, Sarahi Velazquez, sang a solo "A la Orilla de un Palmar" as a serenade to me.

Sarahi has a strong voice and a confident manner. She was well into the heartbreaking story of the poor friendless orphan when, out of nowhere, a wasp started buzzing around her face and microphone and wouldn't leave. Then it landed on her hands. You could have seen it as a yellow-and-black metaphor for all the menacing things and dangers this young Latina would face in life, and how far the venomous world would go to silence her song. Or you could have seen it as just an annoying little insect. Sarahi was a pro. She never flinched or blinked. She kept singing and didn't miss a note. Some people in the audience saw the wasp and got really anxious. Sarahi was cooler than all of them.

Soon enough—too soon!—the bus got us home and we all dispersed from Tucson. The Cenzontles have been incredibly prolific since then, keeping the music going. With them, and all the musical Ronstadts, I am certain that the threads that connect us all are in no danger of breaking. It's the bond that connects Annabelle to Petie and me, and me to my siblings and our dad and mom, and all of us to the wider family web, back as far as any of us can trace. The circle is unbroken, to steal a phrase. One of these days, and it won't be long, we'll rejoin them in a song. It's the songs that keep us connected—that tell us who we are, where we came from, and maybe where we're going. Even when it's dark and scary out. In my great-grandparents' and grandparents' day, other things might have seemed like they would connect us across all generations—the Spanish language, maybe, or our religious faith. But those are no longer the bedrock foundations they used to be.

So I fall back on the music, the unbreakable chain of melody. It hasn't failed us yet.

Also the food. Don't forget the food.

RECIPES

✽ ✽ ✽

JACKIE RONSTADT'S TUNAPEÑOS

Just so you know that this book isn't all about the distant past, I'll mention that not long ago I was watching the excellent series *Fleabag* with Lawrence. It was season two, where Phoebe Waller-Bridge's character falls for an unattainable priest. As we binged the series, I binged on tuna-stuffed jalapeños. This is an Arizonan thing—definitely not a recipe from Grandpa Fred's day—and it's been a Ronstadt family appetizer for years. I learned about them from my sister-in-law Jackie, who married my brother Peter. "What is this gringo food?" I asked her. I was just shocked. I thought, "People are really doing this?" And then I ate one and I went, "Okay, I'm eating up the whole plate."

We call them tunapeños. I told Lawrence that the tuna you get in cans today is no match for the tuna of my childhood—the flavor is insipid, somehow—but he wanted to try anyway. I will admit that his was pretty good, with mayo and chopped onion and pickles. I ate most of them myself.

12 fresh jalapeño peppers

3 cans solid white albacore tuna in olive oil (preferred) or other tuna

½ cup mayonnaise

2 tablespoons Dijon mustard

3 scallions, finely chopped

3 tablespoons dill pickle, diced

1 teaspoon dried dill, or to taste

Salt and pepper to taste

Paprika, for garnish (optional)

Don't knock these till you try 'em.

Slice the peppers lengthwise, remove the seeds and ribs, and set aside. Drain the tuna and, in a medium bowl, combine with the remaining ingredients.

Fill the jalapeño halves with the tuna mixture. Arrange the tunapeños on a platter and sprinkle with paprika, if you like.

EL MINUTO'S CHEESE CRISPS

Cheese crisps are super-sized, super-light, super-simple, and unique to the Tucson area, as far as I know. Restaurants like El Minuto, near the police station downtown, have served them for years, using the extra-large flour tortillas that are common in Tucson and Sonora. When you were young and hungry, mainlining that amount of fat and carbohydrates was so delicious you thought you were going to die of happiness. It would come to the table and you'd think you couldn't eat it all, and then it would be gone in a second. You'd burn your mouth because you couldn't wait for it to cool.

The secret is to make the tortilla crispy *before* putting cheese on it, by frying it in butter or oil. Otherwise it's just melted cheese on a limp tortilla, and who wants that? You have to be able to snap it into pieces. Grab, snap, and shove them in your mouth, letting the butter and cheese drip down your chin.

> 1 10- to 12-inch flour tortilla
>
> ½ cup grated cheese, ideally equal parts Cheddar and Monterey Jack
>
> Vegetable oil for frying
>
> Roasted strips of green chiles, canned or fresh (optional)

Preheat your broiler.

Cover the bottom of a frying pan with about a half-inch of oil, "just enough oil to completely cover the tortilla," as El Minuto's manager Terry Shaar told the *Arizona Daily Star* in 2008. Heat until shimmering but not smoking. Slide the tortilla into the pan and fry it for about 30 seconds, pressing down with a spatula to keep it flat. Remove it to a baking sheet lined with paper towels to drain and get crisp. (You can heat the tortillas on a dry griddle or frying pan, too, if you want to use less fat, but your cheese crisp won't be as good as El Minuto's.)

Top the tortilla with the grated cheese and broil it just until the cheese is melted and bubbly and the tortilla is golden. Remove it from the oven and top with green chile strips, if using. Serve immediately to someone you love, then make another one for yourself.

Cheese crisps are among those things that make Tucson irreplaceable.

GIBBY'S EGGNOG

My grandmother and then my father, known to my family as Gibby, used to make this floating cloud of holiday drunkenness. The original recipe was so big—two dozen eggs, two quarts of milk, two quarts of half-and-half, two pounds of powdered sugar, two quarts of rum, two quarts of brandy—that my sister-in-law Jackie wrote this half-sized recipe.

We were allowed to have a little tiny taste of it when we were small. They told us it was mostly cream—ha. I encountered it again as a grown-up, at my cousin's house at Christmastime. It was so good. It tasted like a health drink, even though it wasn't. It had whipped cream and whipped egg whites floating on the top. The eggs and the milk blended with the liquors, and when you sipped a cup it was like drinking custard.

You could taste all the individual flavors, the fresh nutmeg grated on top. The vanilla was really fragrant, and all that cream. With really good eggs, eggnog can be excellent. I wanted to drink a whole bowl of it, but I couldn't take the liquor. I drank half a cup and had to go home to bed for the rest of the day. It was delicious, but I can't drink alcohol.

12 eggs, separated

1 pound powdered sugar, divided

4 cups dark rum, divided

4 cups brandy, divided

4 cups whole milk

4 cups half-and-half

4 cups whipping cream

3 teaspoons vanilla extract, divided

½ teaspoon cream of tartar

Freshly grated nutmeg, to taste

Separate the egg yolks and whites and then refrigerate the whites. In a large bowl, beat the yolks until very light, gradually adding half of the sugar. Add 2 cups each of the rum and brandy and let stand, covered, for 1 hour. Stir in the milk, half-and-half, cream, 2 teaspoons of vanilla, and the rest of the rum and brandy. Refrigerate at least 3 hours. Remove the egg whites from the refrigerator 1 hour before serving. Shortly before serving, beat the whites with the rest of the sugar, the cream of tartar, and 1 teaspoon of vanilla. Fold the whites gently into the chilled egg-liquor mixture. Serve in glasses with grated nutmeg.

Jim last only make ½   PG 1
GIBBY'S EGGNOG
2 DOZ EGGS — 1< 2 QTS RUM (DARK)
2 QTS MILK (HOMO) — 1< 2 QTS BRANDY
2 QTS ½ + ½   2 TBSP VANILLA
2 QTS WH. CREAM   1 TSP CRM OF TARTAR
2 LBS POWDERED SUGAR   GRATED NUTMEG

BEAT EGG YOLKS TIL VERY NIGHT, GRADUALLY ADD
½ THE SUGAR, THE ½ THE LIQUORS. LET STAND
COVERED ONE HOUR. ADD *+ ½ & ½ & whole milk* WHIPPING CREAM, ½
THE VANILLA, THEN REST OF LIQUORS.
REFRIGERATE AT LEAST 3 HOURS   NEXT PAGE

PG 2
GIBBY'S EGGNOG CON'T

WHEN CLOSE TO SERVING, BEAT EGG WHITES
WITH OTHER ½ OF SUGAR AND 1 TSP
CREAM OF TARTAR. ADD OTHER HALF (ONE
TBSP) OF VANILLA. FOLD INTO CHILLED
MIXTURE, SPRINKLE TOP WITH NUTMEG.

*take egg whites out of fridge
1 hour before beating!*

Here's the unabridged knock-you-flat recipe for Gibby's Eggnog, courtesy of Jackie Ronstadt. That's Suzy's handwriting, with Jackie's note at the bottom.

SONORAN HOT DOGS

There is no definitive account of where the Sonoran hot dog was born, or where and how it crossed the border, or from which direction. The common story, which is highly plausible, is that in the 1980s, a plain old American hot dog migrated to Sonora in search of a better life, and it found that life among the street vendors of Hermosillo. They wrapped it in bacon, nestled it with pinto beans in a soft bolillo roll, and smothered it in Mexican flavor and color, thanks to a barrage of taqueria toppings. Suddenly more interesting and delicious, the Sonoran dog recrossed the border, settling mainly in Tucson.

One of Tucson's best-loved hot dog places is El Güero Canelo, founded by Daniel Contreras. It won a James Beard Foundation Award in 2018. "The Sonoran hot dog," the foundation said, "evinces the flow of culinary and cultural influences from the U.S. to Mexico and back." It's a classic immigrant success story, starring the humble frankfurter. As a German-Mexican-American myself, I couldn't be more proud.

Sonoran hot dogs are easy to make. Start by grilling or broiling a sliced onion, a halved jalapeño, and some whole banana peppers that you have tossed with a little olive oil and salt. Set the peppers and some of the onion aside and make a salsa in a food processor or blender: ¼ cup of the onion, plus the jalapeño, a cup of chopped cilantro, a smashed garlic clove, and a couple tablespoons of lime juice.

Wrap the hot dogs in bacon slices and grill, broil, or fry. (Toothpicks can help hold the bacon in place.) Spread cooked pinto beans in split-top hot-dog buns, and top with the works—the grilled onions, jalapeño salsa, chopped tomatoes, diced chiles, radish slices, avocado, Mexican crema, mayonnaise, mustard. Using squeeze bottles to make a thin, ribbony lattice of mayo, mustard, and other goopy toppings, hiding the dog completely, will make it look authentically Sonoran. Serve with the banana peppers and lots of napkins.

Somewhere under that avalanche of toppings is a hot dog wrapped in bacon. It's all too much, which is why it's so good.

Mischief, the appaloosa I had as a girl, was kind, caring, and really smart. She became a brood mare, which meant she got to live out her life in a pasture, eating apples and having babies, which is a better ending than most horses get.

10
CODA: MY DREAM

I DREAMED I WAS BACK HOME IN TUCSON with Suzy, Peter, Mike, and my mom and dad. We were at our house at East Prince Road and Jackson Avenue.

We were in the backyard, and all on horseback. Suzy was on Barley Dew, her knotheaded palomino mare. I was on Mischief, my dear, sweet appaloosa, who died many years ago. We also had some horses from Pete Martinez's place, the rodeo arena and riding stable near our house. They were for Mike, Peter, and our mom and dad to ride.

We were next to the house, out where my mother had a rose garden, by the eucalyptus trees. It was probably like 10 a.m. or so, or maybe noon. Whenever it was, we didn't have much time. We had to leave, for some urgent reason; I don't know what. We had to hurry up. We were running for our lives.

Everybody was saddled up and loaded with gear. We had saddlebags packed with provisions and rolled-up blankets and rifles in scabbards. It was clearly going to be a long trip.

The plan was to head north, through the mesquite and palo verde, to the Rillito River, and then turn east and follow the river as far as we could go.

The Rillito is dry most of the year, flat and sandy, so it would be a relatively easy ride, at least at first. We'd keep the mountains to our left—the Santa Catalinas and then the Rincons—and turn gradually south. The path on a map, ruling out the interstate highways and using dream logic where necessary, would take us into the mountains to Canelo, and then over the border, to the old mining town of Cananea, the headwaters of the Río Sonora, and then down the length of the river valley, winding between canyons, along the green floodplain, down through time, into the past, down into the heart of Sonora. ❖

A panorama of the Mustang Mountains in southeast Arizona. Their upper slopes are ecologically distinct habitats called "sky islands."

A NOTE FROM LINDA ON THE MUSIC

The songs mentioned in this book, like the recipes, are only the briefest sampling of what you could spend a Sonoran lifetime exploring. This list is not encyclopedic or authoritative—it's just songs that are dear to me, that evoke a special place and time. You can hear them on a playlist available on all major streaming services. A CD and digital compilation of many of these songs can also be had from the label Putumayo; *Feels Like Home: Songs from the Sonoran Borderlands—Linda Ronstadt's Musical Odyssey* can be ordered from retailers or at putumayo.com.

SONGS WE RONSTADTS LOVED AND SANG

"El Sueño" (The Dream)

My brothers, Peter and Mike, sang this beautiful huapango folk song with me on my record *Mas Canciones*. We learned the harmonies as kids from a record by Trío Tariácuri, three brothers who were beloved musicians in Mexico for decades, starting in the 1930s.

"Mi Ranchito" (My Little Farm)

This is the song that best expresses how I feel about my childhood home. It's about returning in memory to the little plot of land where you grew up, which in my case is a place with horses, chickens, goats, dogs, and whatever else turned up, including peacocks and coatimundis.

"El Crucifijo de Piedra" (The Stone Crucifix)

I learned this huapango from the version sung by Miguel Aceves Mejía, the ranchera idol and actor. In it, an abandoned lover stands alone and crying in front of a church, so sad that the crucified Christ cries, too. It's one of the most beautiful songs in the literature.

"Lo Siento Mi Vida" (I'm Sorry My Love)

Kenny Edwards and I wrote this with my dad. Kenny wanted it to be all in Spanish, but after he wrote the first line, we needed help for the rest. We told my dad what we wanted to say, and the song came together in a three-way phone conversation.

"La Calandria" (The Songbird)

This is a naughty song that Peter, Mike, and I used to sing. It made us giggle. Singing it in Spanish somehow made it seem not quite as dirty, with its lines about love and women's petticoats and things that happen in men's undershorts.

"Y Andale" (Get On with It)

I recorded this with my niece Mindy when she was fifteen. She sang it so well, with lovely innocence, even though it's about drunken debauchery. Our version was a hit in Mexico City.

"Ragtime Cowboy Joe"

We kids used to sing this in three-part harmony in the car. Our mom would sing it with us, too. I didn't hear a recording of it until I was an adult. I like the version by the Sons of the Pioneers.

"A la Orilla de un Palmar" (At the Edge of a Palm Grove)

This is one of those songs that's a time tunnel back to childhood, with Peter, Suzy, Mike, and me singing in the back seat of the family car, or in the kitchen, our hands in the dishwater. Mike also sang it in a trio with our cousins John and Bill. It's about a poor orphan alone in the world.

"Blue Shadows"

Peter learned this cowboy song in his boys' chorus and then taught it to our brother Mike and our cousins John and Bill. Those three performed often as the Ronstadt Cousins, and this song was a good showcase for the family blend of voices.

"Canadian Moon"

My brother Mike wrote and recorded this with his band, Ronstadt Generations. It's my favorite song of his. It came to him in Canada, naturally, where everything is so green and lush it can make a homesick Tucsonan cry. This song shows the hold the desert can have on you.

"Barrio Viejo" (Old Neighborhood)

The great Chicano bandleader and songwriter Lalo Guerrero never forgot how Tucson bulldozed and buried his old neighborhood in the 1960s, in the name of urban renewal. In 1990, this song brought it back to life. He was in his seventies then, still working at the top of his talent, and this may be his greatest song.

"Los Chucos Suaves" (The Cool Dudes)

This song was a hit in the 1940s, when Lalo was in his prime as a bandleader. The trumpet player and piano player on his recording of this song—about young, hip Chicanos in Los Angeles dancing and getting drunk—are particularly skilled.

"La Burrita" (The Little Donkey)

I never heard this on a record when I was little; I knew it from singing it myself and having it sung to me—including once by Lalo and my dad serenading me on my third birthday in the traditional Mexican way, at two in the morning.

"I Never Will Marry"

Dolly Parton and I both love this song and recorded it together. According to Ronstadt family rules, this was my sister's song, because she was the first of us to sing it. But Suzy married three times, so it became mine.

"Old Paint"

We always used to sing this old cowboy song as kids. We never heard it on a record; it was just there, in the air. "The song smells of saddle leather," Carl Sandburg wrote of it in his 1927 folk-music anthology, *The American Songbag*. He said it came "from a buckaroo who was last heard of as heading for the Border with friends in both Tucson and El Paso." For my version on the record

Simple Dreams, I played guitar myself, in my uniquely incompetent style.

"Adonde Voy" (Where Am I Going?)

Tish Hinojosa, the Texas singer and songwriter, wrote this song about hope, love, and loneliness. A fugitive on the run from immigration misses home and worries about a lover left behind. I sang it on a record called *Winter Light*.

"Dreams of the San Joaquin"

This is about a migrant worker in the San Joaquin Valley in Dust Bowl days—a song of desperate times in a beautiful, bountiful land. Jack Wesley Routh and Randy Sharp wrote it, and a Ronstadt family chorus joined me on the record: my siblings, Suzy, Peter, and Mike; my cousins Johnny and Bill; and my niece Mindy.

SONGS OF MEXICO AND THE BORDERLANDS

"Flor Silvestre" (Wild Flower)

It's hard to describe the way the great Trío Calaveras sing an old folk tune like this. They have such beautiful harmonies. When the Indigenous rhythm of the huapango meets the almost military precision of their joined voices, the effect is mystical.

"Por un Amor" (For a Love)

I adore Lucha Reyes's version of this song. She was the first of Mexico's great women ranchera singers, and she has not been matched. She started out as an opera singer but damaged her vocal cords and lost her operatic voice. It became husky—perfect for ranchera music.

"Cucurrucucú Paloma" (The Cooing Dove)

This is Lola Beltrán's signature song. It's gorgeous and full of passion, and she sings it to perfection. Like many huapangos, there's a lot of falsetto in it, which is hard to do. A song like this is usually sung by a man, but Lola proved that women can sing falsetto beautifully, too.

"La Mariquita" (The Ladybug)

Amalia Mendoza, sister to the members of Trío Tariácuri, was considered the most musically precise of the ranchera singers. She was known for this traditional song. It's a son, similar in its rhythm pattern to a huapango. The singer asks a young woman, the little ladybug, to "cover me with your shawl, because I'm freezing to death."

"Paloma Negra" (Black Dove)

If I had heard Chavela Vargas sing this ranchera song or anything else when I was growing up, I would have changed my whole singing style. Songwriters loved her because she was so musical—she could interpret a song just as they had intended it, with its full emotional reading. Her version of this sorrowful song is unbeatable. She *owns* it.

"Malagueña Salerosa" (Enchanting Woman from Málaga)

Here's another thrilling huapango, romantic and passionate. The Trío Calaveras sang it beautifully. It can be hard to pull off, with all its falsetto parts, but my brother Peter did it well.

"Plegaría Guadalupana"
(Guadalupe Prayer)

The Trío Tariácuri's vocal style was featured beautifully in their recording of this song. It reflects many Mexicans' devotion to Our Lady of Guadalupe, who by Catholic tradition appeared to the peasant Juan Diego in 1531. (You don't often hear the backstory: that Juan Diego was actually an Aztec priest, and that the spot where he claimed to have seen the Virgin had once been a shrine to Tonantzin, the Aztecs' Mother Earth, who made the corn grow. In other words, Mexico's patron saint is an Indigenous goddess in disguise, which is why I love her.)

"El Camino" (The Path)

This one's sort of spooky. The Trío Tariácuri sing it in a yodeling falsetto style. It's about traveling long distances through the night on horseback, and the daunting things you encounter. Their voices sound mysterious, almost supernatural.

"El Hielo (ICE)"

This song is by a Los Angeles band I love, La Santa Cecilia. Its lead singer, La Marisoul, has the most interesting voice I've heard in years. The title is a play on words: "Hielo" is Spanish for "ice," and ICE is the acronym for Immigration and Customs Enforcement. The song is a sensitive representation of the true human cost of unfair immigration laws.

SONGS FROM LOS CENZONTLES AND FRIENDS

"Sonora Querida" (Beloved Sonora)

Los Cenzontles recorded this with David Hidalgo of Los Lobos. Many consider it the unofficial state song of Sonora.

"Ojitos Negros" (Little Black Eyes)

Los Cenzontles sang this traditional Mexican song on their 2008 album, *Songs of Wood and Steel*, and then again on *San Patricio*, a 2010 album by the Chieftains and Ry Cooder. Their a cappella treatment is amazingly rich and pure.

"La Manta" (The Blanket), "Arenita Azul" (Blue Sands), "El Torero" (The Bullfighter), "Naninan Upirin" (How Will I Do It)

These four traditional songs are part of the repertoire of Los Cenzontles' youth group, Los Cenzontles Juvenil, made up of kids age eight to sixteen. They start young, absorbing deep traditions and rhythms, and learning to sing in both Spanish and Mexican Indigenous languages, of which there are sixty-eight. They can really play. "La Manta" is a son jarocho from Veracruz; "Arenita Azul" is a chilena from Oaxaca; "El Torero" is a son abajeño from Jalisco; and "Naninan Upirin" is a son abajeño from the P'urhépecha Indigenous people living in the Michoacán region.

"The Dreamer"

When I introduced Jackson Browne to Eugene Rodriguez and his cultural organization Los Cenzontles, I felt they would hit it off. Jackson and Eugene soon teamed up to write this beautiful song, about a family divided by the border and our unjust immigration laws.

"Somebody Please"

This soulful lowrider standard from the late '60s was made popular by Manuel (Big Manny) Gonzales, who had a band in East L.A. called the Blazers. He was a really good singer. In 2021, Los Cenzontles, La Mari-soul, and David Hidalgo and Cesar Rosas of Los Lobos sang it as a tribute to Big Manny, who died in 2016.

"Los Hermanos" (The Brothers)

This is an example of how Los Cenzontles reaches out to the greater community—in this case the San Francisco Symphony. Sometimes when you load classical players onto traditional songs and styles, it doesn't quite work, but this collaboration was very successful. I admire the way Los Cenzontles can find ways to build on and revitalize old traditions, as in this song about the bonds that connect migrants of many countries, united by the perilous journey north to the United States: "I have so many brothers that I can't count them all."

"Voy Caminando" (I Go Walking)

Eugene Rodriguez wrote this song about a migrant's journey toward his dream. "Tomorrow I go walking / There is nothing more for me here / That is why I am looking / For my future on the horizon." The rhythm is provided by the dancers' feet.

"La Pelota" (The Ball)

Eugene also wrote this political tune, dis-guising it as a song about soccer. The ball is a metaphor for how Mexican Americans are kicked this way and that, side to side, up and down, by politicians and others who take them for granted. It's a great song, and I love its driving rhythm.

Agaves with the Huachuca Mountains in the background, near Canelo.

GRATITUDE

LINDA: I want to thank my co-conspirators Lawrence and Bill for helping me turn the ghost of my great-grandmother into the foundation for a book. Lawrence has shown great empathy as a collaborator and brought discipline plus organizational and research skills to this project that I am sorely lacking. He and his wife, Pat, have been excellent traveling companions during the times we ran the road between Tucson and Banámichi, and Pat has been most helpful with feedback during this entire process. Bill and Athena Steen and their sons, Benito, Oso, and Panther, have been an inspiration to me since the late 1980s, when I first encountered the Canelo Project. Bill's beautiful images of the Sonoran Desert and beyond are informed by a deep knowledge of the culture and people of this region. His network of contacts in Sonora also made an invaluable contribution to this book. I'm particularly grateful to Bill's friends, the superb cooks Armida Contreras and Lupita Madero, for their contributions to the recipes. Bill, too, is a fine hand in the kitchen and added his ideas to our culinary collection.

LAWRENCE: Linda invited me on this trip, and our journey together was a joy. I have never had a better colleague and writing partner. Ry Cooder introduced me to Los Cenzontles and thus to Linda; I'm in his debt. Any desert would be lucky to be photographed by Bill Steen. Jack Sherman inspired the title. My most existential thanks go to Zak and Sophie and to my love and inspiration in all things, Pat.

WE COULD NOT HAVE MADE THIS BOOK WITHOUT THE HELP OF MANY PEOPLE. THESE THANK-YOUS ARE FROM BOTH OF US:

Janet Stark, Linda's assistant, gave this project sanity, clarity, and momentum. She always kept us moving through choppy waters, refusing to let us drown. John Boylan, Linda's friend, manager, and co-conspirator of many decades, also was lifesaving.

Steve Wasserman, Heyday's publisher, championed this project; we are grateful for his enthusiasm, calm guidance, and unflagging support. His colleagues Marthine Satris, who edited the words; Diane Lee, who handled the art direction and photos; Ashley Ingram, who did the design; and Gayle Wattawa, who guided the project to completion, are professionals of the highest caliber. So are the others on Heyday's team: Emmerich Anklam, Christopher Miya, Marlon Rigel, and Kalie Caetano, and our publicist, Megan Beatie. Lisa K. Marietta, our copy editor, steered us toward clarity and grace and away from error. Copy editors are among the finest human beings we know, raising up other people's words as firmly and lovingly as if the words were their own. The world can learn from their dedication and selflessness.

Erin Hosier of Dunow, Carlson & Lerner Literary Agency piloted this project with patience, tact, and great expertise. We learned so much from her. Professor Cynthia Radding shared her deep knowledge of Sonora's history and peoples and graciously repaired weaknesses in the text. Bob Vint helped us better understand Tucson's history, neighborhoods, and architectural landmarks, especially the San Xavier del Bac mission. We're grateful for his kindness (and Spanish fluency). Gary Paul Nabhan, Jesús García, and Dena Cowan lent their expertise on desert plants and agriculture. Carlos Quintero translated Linda's great-grandmother's letters into English from Spanish. Perri Pyle and Rachael Black helped us dig into Ronstadt family history at the Arizona History Museum. Dan Guerrero offered invaluable information about his dad, Lalo Guerrero, and his song "Barrio Viejo." Diego Javier Piña Lopez showed us Casa Alitas. Joseph (Bob) Diaz and Patricia Ballesteros at the University of Arizona Libraries helped us obtain an archival image. Carolyn Robinson kindly granted permission to use a Ronstadt family photo by her father, the great Arizona photographer Ray Manley.

Peter and Jackie Ronstadt, Petie and Jackie Ronstadt, Bobby George Ronstadt, Jim Ronstadt, Katya Peterson, Eugene Rodriguez and Marie-Astrid Do Rodriguez, Deb and Dennis Moroney, Chris Newman, Pablo Alvarado, and Shura Wallin were gracious collaborators who freely shared their time, stories, and insights. Of the many friends and colleagues who supplied inspiration and encouragement, essential introductions, and constructive ideas, we're especially thankful to CC Goldwater, Robert Stieve, Julie Just, Teresa Bruce, Abby Aguirre, Brooke Larson, Carol Giacomo, Steven Greenhouse, Ciarán ÓGaora, and Mark Bittman.

BILL: My love and appreciation to the people of the Rio Sonora who not only gave me access to their lives, but gave me the acceptance that made both my photos in this book possible as well as the Sonoran recipes. They have taught me much about life as well as the place that I live. Listing their names, an impossible task, they are far too numerous.

Of course Linda, without whom I would not be part of this book.

PERMISSIONS AND CREDITS

All images by Bill Steen with the exception of the following:

Photos on pages vi, xix, 5 (left), 90, 92 (top and middle), 95, 96, 100, 103 (top), 110, 187 (both), and 200 courtesy of Linda Ronstadt's personal collection.

Photo on page viii courtesy of Arizona Historical Society, PC 1000, General Photo Collection, Portrait-Ronstadt, Frederick A., #74075.

Map on page xxii: Herman Ehrenberg, Map of the Gadsden Purchase: Sonora and portions of New Mexico, Chihuahua & California. Cincinnati, Ohio: Middleton, Strobridge & Co., 1858. Image courtesy of the Library of Congress, https://www.loc.gov/item/98686018/.

Photos on pages 5 (right), 58, 79, 83, 86 (both), and 98 courtesy of Arizona Historical Society, Ronstadt Family collection, MS 0695, Box 11., Folders 2, 12, and 15.

Photo on page 44 courtesy of Special Collections, the University of Arizona.

Lithograph on page 44: Papagos, ca. 1857, by Arthur Schott, with Sarony, Major & Knapp (lithography studio). Image courtesy of the Library of Congress, https://www.loc.gov/item/awhbib000070/.

Image on page 48 by Lollesgard Specialty Co., Tucson, courtesy of Lawrence Downes.

Image on page 68 courtesy of Arizona Historical Society, Ronstadt Family collection, MS 0695, Box 2, Folder 4.

Photo on page 70 courtesy of Arizona Historical Society, Western Ways collection, MS 1255, Photo Negatives Group C, Box 3.

Photos on page 75 and 92 (bottom) courtesy of Arizona Historical Society, Ronstadt Family collection, MS 0695, Box 17, Folders 3 and 6.

Image on page 77 courtesy of Arizona Historical Society, Ronstadt Family collection, MS 0695, Box 2, Folder 3.

Photo on page 94 by Ray Manley, courtesy of his daughter Carolyn Robinson.

Photo on page 108 courtesy of Katya Peterson.

Photo on page 113 courtesy of Dan Guerrero.

Photo on page 129 by Lawrence Downes.

Photo on page 162 (top) by Amy Dodd, courtesy of Bill Steen.

Photo on page 176 by Rosa Angelica Sarabia.

Photo on pages 178–179 by Verenice Velazquez.

Photo on page 185 by Armando Quintero.

Photo on page 197 courtesy of Jackie Ronstadt.

Photo on page 218 by Kalin Steen.

"A La Orilla De Un Palmar" by Manuel M. Ponce. Copyright © 1945 Promotora Hispano Americana de Musica, S.A. Administered by Peer International Corporation for the World. All rights reserved. Used by permission.

"Barrio Viejo," words and music by Lalo Guerrero. Lyric reprinted by permission of Barrio Libre Music (BMI).

"El Sueno" by Nicandro Castillo. Copyright © 1947 Promotora Hispano Americana de Musica, S.A. Administered by Peer International Corporation for the World. All rights reserved. Used by permission.

"Feels Like Home," words and music by Randy Newman. Copyright © 1996 Randy Newman Music (ASCAP). All rights reserved. Used by permission of Alfred Music.

"Lo Siento Mi Vida," words and music by Gilbert Ronstadt, Kenny Edwards, and Linda Ronstadt. © Normal Music. Courtesy of Normal Music.

ABOUT THE AUTHORS

LINDA RONSTADT is one of the most versatile singers of our era. Her four-decade recording career encompassed country, rock-and-roll, the Great American Songbook, jazz, opera, Broadway standards, Mexican and tropical music, and Americana. Her worldwide album sales totaled more than fifty million, with at least thirty-one gold and platinum records. She has won ten Grammy Awards, is a recipient of the National Medal of Arts, and is a member of the Rock and Roll Hall of Fame. She serves on the advisory board of Los Cenzontles Cultural Arts Academy, which has taught Mexican folk music, dance, and art to children in the San Francisco Bay Area for more than three decades.

Linda is the daughter of Ruth Mary and Gilbert Ronstadt of Tucson, the granddaughter of Mexican immigrants to Arizona, and a descendant of Spanish settlers in northern Sonora, Mexico. Her 2013 book, *Simple Dreams: A Musical Memoir*, was a *New York Times* best seller. She lives in San Francisco.

LAWRENCE DOWNES is a writer and editor in New York. For more than thirty years he worked in newspapers, including the *Chicago Sun-Times*, *Newsday*, and the *New York Times*. At the *Times* he was an editor and member of the editorial board, and he wrote about immigration, New York city and state politics and government, disability rights, veterans affairs, the environment, and other subjects. He wrote *There Is Just Us: Special Olympics Rising*, a 2019 book about the Special Olympics movement and the global struggle for human rights for people with intellectual and developmental disabilities. His op-eds and essays have appeared in the *Washington Post*, the *Los Angeles Times*, the *Honolulu Star-Advertiser*, and other newspapers. He lives in Northport, New York, with his wife, the journalist Patricia Wiedenkeller.

ABOUT THE PHOTOGRAPHER

BILL STEEN has been photographing, exploring, learning, and sharing the beauty and bounty of the Sonoran borderlands for more than three decades. With his wife, Athena Swentzell Steen, he is a founder of the Canelo Project, near Elgin, Arizona, a family-based community and an applied educational center that gives people hands-on experience with a lifestyle that aims to be sustainable. It is an ongoing exploration of living, growing food, and building, in a way that creates friendship, beauty, and simplicity. The Steens are the authors, with David Bainbridge, of *The Straw Bale House* and numerous other books about straw-bale construction and sustainable living.